TWENTY-FIVE
YEARS IN
KASHMIR

TWENTY-FIVE YEARS IN KASHMIR

Headmaster on a Mission

JOHN RAY

Signal Books
Oxford

This edition first published in the UK in 2019 by
Signal Books Limited
36 Minster Road
Oxford OX4 1LY
www.signalbooks.co.uk

A catalogue record for this book is available from the British Library

ISBN 978-1-909930-78-0 Cloth

Cover Design: Tora Kelly
Typesetting: Tora Kelly
Cover Image: ImagesofIndia/Shutterstock; Catherine Ray

Printed in India by Imprint Press

For

This is written for the young people of Kashmir. For the fortunate, such as the old students of Biscoe and Mallinson, who can 'make a difference' for all. For the unfortunate, lacking hope and misled, who throw stones at the police, that they may find hope. For peace and true azadi *for all, including the administrators and the police. For teachers everywhere.*

Apologia

Memory fades. I have kept diaries, but not exhaustive notes. Opinions, errors and omissions are mine alone. I have changed a very few names where an identity needed to be shielded. More fundamentally, I can only write as an English person of my generation: I grew up when a vast Empire painted the world's maps red. I have sought to understand the world we all now inhabit and ask forgiveness for perceived traces of cultural imperialism.

CONTENTS

PREFACE TO UK EDITION

This book, published by ISPCK in Delhi last year, was written mainly for the old students of two famous nineteenth-century mission schools in Srinagar, the ancient capital of Kashmir. It looks back to the very happy quarter century from 1962 to 1986 during which my wife and I brought up our family within a stone's throw of Lal Chowk, the tumultuous centre of that unique Valley.

The UK edition is in response to friends who want it available here, a range of people interested in 'Kashmir'. It does not deal with the political or religious scene, but is simply a slice of 'life as it was', or at least as I saw it.

Books on Kashmir and its trials are many, but for those whose appetite is whetted by this one, I would recommend two. *The Missionary and the Maharajas* by Dr Hugh Tyndale Biscoe (Tauris, 2019) gives a fascinating and authoritative account of an extraordinary work, telling us the good and the not-so-good of the age CE Tyndale Biscoe lived through. His grandson, avoiding the traps of family hagiography, will enlighten critics, whether secular or Christian, of 'mission' in the imperial age.

My Kashmir (Penguin, 2014) by Wajahat Habibullah, formerly Chairman of India's National Commission for Minorities and earlier Kashmir's senior civil servant in terrible times, has much to teach us all in today's frenetic search for identity.

FOREWORD

Memories. This is an account of a time past set in an emerging society, an emerging time imbued with an indefinable emotion that can be described variously as fascination, nostalgia, or indeed high romance but is in fact simply the expression of a deep love felt for an institution, and understanding for a people. This is Ray's book penned by the best representative of an era in which Kashmir emerged from a state of abject subjection to a sometimes benevolent despotism under a colonial heel into a modern Indian state. It covers the emergence of a new political hierarchy, the rise of a new ruling and middle class and most of all new generations of youth who will lead the state into its future. And although Ray places much hope in the boys and girls emerging from Tyndale Biscoe and its sister school the Mallinson, I fear that I, a former administrator of the state in a time of crisis, cannot share that hope even though I dare to share the dream. Couched in prose the work is poetry in which, although each chapter follows the last in sequence, each can be read as an independent reverie. Writing of the school post 1954, beset with a decline triggered by the unhappy exit of its then Principal Dr Edmonds, Ray writes that 'The large under-used area of invaluable ground ... set in the growing commercial area of the city, awaited development. I remember a sense of surprise that no-one had seized it, and a dawning realisation that the reputation and status of the School was such as to make this impossible.' Sadly, today and more so after the flooding of the city in 2014, that regard for tradition, or indeed for all the beauty of Kashmir's heritage, is part of an already distant past. Tyndale Biscoe sits today amidst a high cost, unsightly commercial area, the pavements along its walls under threat of encroachment, with its present Principal Parwez Kaul locked in an unceasing crusade to protect a historic legacy. Even so, in reward for Kaul's constant guard, within those walls the Tyndale Biscoe and Mallinson remain what Ray describes as 'a green oasis of quiet'. There can be no better tribute to his evocation of Kashmir than placing it in reference to the popular nineteenth-century poem of one of Ray's own countrymen who had never visited Kashmir but immersed himself in the legend, which Ray, by bringing to life in this beautiful work, attests to having actually been.

Who has not heard of the Vale of Cashmere,
With its roses the brightest that earth ever gave...
Like a bride, full of blushes, when lingering to take
A last look of her mirror at night ere she goes!
When the shrines through the foliage are gleaming half
* shown,*
And each hallows the hour by some rites of its own.
Here the music of prayer from a minaret swells,
Here the magian his urn, full of perfume, is swinging,
And here, at the altar, a zone of sweet bells
Round the waist of some fair Indian dancer is ringing.
Or to see it by moonlight,—when mellowly shines
The light o'er its palaces, gardens, and shrines;
When the waterfalls gleam, like a quick fall of stars,
And the nightingale's hymn from the Isle of Chenars
Is broken by laughs and light echoes of feet
From the cool, shining walks where the young people meet.[1]

---

1   Thomas Moore (1779-1852), 'The Light of the Harem'.

The birdsong of nightingales still rustles the chenars and weeping willow and prancing youth meet on cool walks. But will we ever again see that Kashmir, in which Tyndale Biscoe nestled in its infancy? Or will Ray's own poetic ramblings be an elegy to lost times? The answer to that question remains, of course, in large part with the fortunate young of Kashmir for whom the author writes.

Wajahat Habibullah

INTRODUCTION

In 1956, while climbing with two friends in the Swiss Alps, Andy fell to his death as a rock tipped over and carried him down eight hundred feet. He was by far the best climber among us and one of the finest men I have known.

This is a little book of stories of our good times in Kashmir. But how should a young teacher from England find himself in Sheikh Bagh? When Andy fell that day in 1956 above Arolla in Switzerland my cosy world was shattered. I remember praying. 'God, if there is a God, why did Andy die?' Sometimes a death, even a tragic and unnecessary death like Andy's, changes things. Andy's death was the reason I landed in Kashmir six years later.

One's ninetieth birthday, if one is so fortunate, is a good milestone to look out on life, and to reflect in the age of the internet and social media. What are we doing here on earth for a hairsbreadth of time? If we believe in God, what is He saying to His world today? If we don't, then how do we make sense of our times?

After a succession of challenges which were all good preparation, I was privileged to work as Principal of the Tyndale-Biscoe School from 1962 to 1986. The Biscoe and Mallinson schools had played a leading part in opening the door to modernity on what in 1880 was a society virtually unchanged since medieval times, and they are now at the centre of a complex of five schools with eight thousand pupils. Canon Tyndale-Biscoe and Miss Muriel Mallinson were key figures in that process and remained high in the affections of many Kashmiris when my wife and I, newly married, arrived in Srinagar in January 1962.

It so happened that our quarter century there coincided with what was probably the happiest period in Kashmir's long dark history. For that short space of time, between the poverty and obscurantisms of the past and the tragic events of the last thirty years, there was a clear sense and expectation of progress, democracy and material improvement among very many people in the Valley of Kashmir. My successor Mr Parwez Samuel Kaul has asked me to write this book to give to the leaving students of the Biscoe and Mallinson Schools a picture of life in the Schools during those years. Mr and Mrs Kaul still live in the house we built in 1966 and have been responsible for the Schools at Sheikh Bagh for over thirty tumultuous years. They, like us, are links in the chain of guardians of unique institutions.

I have chosen to do this in the form of a memoir, a reflection on some of the relationships, the personalities and the happenings that in retrospect seem significant in the life of the school and of Srinagar during those years, before they are swept from living memory. I am stretching Mr Kaul's request to think of the leaving students of my time, thirty or forty years ago. We last met some of you at the Mallinson School Centenary in 2012, and I met others at an Old Boys' reunion in Dubai in 2014. Today it is a different world from that of half a century ago. Many have lived through bitter traumas of life in Srinagar, especially in the time after December 1989, and even more recently. Many also are refugees in their own country. Even those who have successfully rebuilt their lives mourn the loss of their unique ancestral homeland. Many others have enjoyed good times and prosperity. We all see the past in the light of the more recent. So, I tend to see those good days in the light of all I have experienced since.

Just as our schools have been at the heart of change in society in the past, our hope is that they may yet contribute to new springs of life in the future.

When we re-visited Kashmir after a nineteen-year absence in 2005, I commented to a fifteen-year-old village boy in the Tangmarg branch school that we sensed a new spirit in the Valley. His eyes lit up: 'It's renaissance!' he exclaimed. I could not have imagined a Kashmiri village boy so aptly using that term from European history a generation earlier. Again, in our last visit in 2012 we were especially impressed, in the Girls' School, by a widespread looking forward to better times. Could it be the women who will lead the way to peace in Kashmir, the men having been unable to do so? Worldwide the breaking down of male dominance and the accession to education, power and leadership of women is beginning to affect culture, religion and the whole fabric of life. There is only one short chapter here on the Girls' School, as my duties and memories are mainly of the Boys' Senior School, but there is no doubting the central importance of women's education, in Kashmir as elsewhere.

Writing thus in the form of a reflection, the intent is that, while one sees through the microcosm of a school and city, what is written may be of interest to a wider public concerned for the unique Valley of Kashmir. In 2019 it remains one of the very difficult issues for the world's leaders.

Since our last visit there has again been a periodic relapse into cycles of violence and reaction, even more destructive than the floods of 2014. There are perhaps two reasons which lead children and teenagers to pelt the police with stones: hopelessness and indoctrination for a 'higher cause'. That the eight thousand children who attend our schools have not in the past few years been among them may indicate that they are among the fortunate minority who have hope of a good future. Not only in Kashmir is the mix of radical politicised religion with local injustice and grievance a recipe for catastrophe. It doesn't have to be like that. The genius of Kashmiri people is very different. What role do the fortunate among us have in extending hope where none exists?

There is no one panacea for those who have suffered much and have, it sometimes seems, ceased to hope for civic peace. Yet I dare to hope, even in this recollection of times which were good and hopeful, that there may be an encouragement to those who, in the words of scripture, 'seek peace and pursue it'. We can all do that. Even while political troubles continue, life must go on, and to sustain their families many Kashmiris have moved out. This is nothing new. Not so long ago the poor would leave their frozen fields to earn a pittance as coolies in Punjab cities through the winter months, and the salesmen of Kashmir handicrafts have in recent times become known throughout India, and indeed worldwide. Yet even those who flourish in professional or business life in the Gulf or further afield cherish their family homes in Zainakadal or Nishat, and return, whether to visit or in retirement. Thus, there is a kind of cross fertilisation between the Valley and the wider world. Can this work for the common good? How, for instance, can our old students best contribute?

All this sounds very serious. The stories that make up this book are mainly of small events, the stuff of our lives in Srinagar, or of people of little importance except to their families. But the history of our schools, and even its reflection in the 'Six Chief Ministers' section of these pages, is a reminder that our small efforts can contribute for good to prevail in the wider picture.

Some readers will hurry to matters such as these and may be impatient of references to loved and respected teachers. Others may have little interest in political figures of a bygone age and want more personal detail. But Kashmir, and especially the Srinagar establishment, is a family uniquely bound by multiple relationships, one which we have been privileged to know quite closely. Today's multiple relational networks can be a decisive force for good.

I could not have offered this to the public, even to our tolerant old students, without the understanding and knowledge of two distinguished friends. Dr Mohammed Ishaq Khan, who in 1978 presented me with a copy of his History of Srinagar, 1846 to 1947, is my authority for comments on education and social change, and especially his fair and judicious assessment of the contribution of CMS missionaries, particularly Tyndale Biscoe and Miss Mallinson. As a foreigner, however involved, I would not have dared to comment so frankly on aspects of traditional Srinagar society without reference to his authoritative work. His wife Mahmooda, who has now also sadly passed away, for long taught in our primary school, and his children are also ours.

When I listened to Wajahat Habibullah, the then Chair of India's National Commission for Minorities, during our 2012 visit, I wished that he could have been employed also in Britain during the emergence of the ideology of multi-culturalism, where my country has made many mistakes. If only India had listened more readily to his wisdom, the course of events in Srinagar in the period after we left in October 1986 could have been happier. His *My Kashmir* is subtitled 'the Dying of the Light', yet it makes clear, with the authority of one who repeatedly risked his life in Srinagar, that there is still no fundamental reason to prevent Kashmiris recovering peace and dignity within India's broad bounds. He has enriched this small offering by kindly adding a foreword.

I am also indebted to Dr Jyoti Sahi, whose art is world renowned, for his series of line drawings which add grace to this little book and remind us of the balance and beauty of the

Kashmir scene as it was before the torrent of 'development.' The series of pictures, originally intended to accompany a School book of prayers which was never completed, portrays in Kashmiri style and dress the story of Zacchaeus, the rich tax collector who, meeting Jesus, gave away half his wealth and reaped a richer reward. Given Wajahat's perception of the background role of corruption leading to the breakdown of 1989, we need more to do their part, large or small, in cleaning up the public life of Kashmir.

As we recall those happy days in the beautiful campus of Sheikh Bagh, whether as children or as teachers, and think of the personalities, perhaps of Mr Sat Lal, or Miss Carol Hitter, or of some memory like the Dal Cross or the Mahadev climb—of all the sheer fun that we had—it's for others to judge if some of this has echoes of something more, if it has made an impress of generosity of character and has strengthened our lives not only for our good but equally for the good of others. This might be a strange idea for some, but it was the spring of those who founded this School and have taken it forward.

Kashmir has always been at a junction, between areas of different faiths, languages and cultures. It is four hundred miles, just an hour by plane, from Delhi, but only three hundred from Kabul or from Yarkand in Chinese Sinkiang. Our School, too, was a meeting point and a melting pot (to mix the metaphors) of all kinds of influences.

In those days a few of the 'ancient Britons' were still around. Later came the riddle of the hippies, who had thrown away the riches of the West to embrace eastern mysticism, or cheap *charas*, or both. Then we had as a School, a succession of notable bishops as chairmen, and always a few notably 'different' teachers from other parts of India, such as the scholarly Dr Thakurdas. The young short-term volunteers from UK made a valuable bridge between our worlds, and the last of the foreign missionaries, Mr and Mrs Nickless, Miss Morgan and, in the Girls' School, Miss Gravelle, will be warmly remembered by those who knew them. Miss Margaret Shaw, Froebel trained head of the Primary School earlier, was a link back to the wartime School run in parallel to the Mission School by Mr and Mrs Eric Biscoe.

Mrs Ray and I were, of course. also members of the Christian community, which itself was totally cross cultural. Members of All Saints Church included engineering students from Nagaland whose grandparents might have been head hunters, as well as Keralites, whose Christian heritage went back to St Thomas the apostle of Jesus, and who tended to view western Christians as newcomers.

As with music, so with writing, there is often both a major and a minor key. It is over thirty years since we left Srinagar, and many of our old students are spread across the world. Like me, since leaving Kashmir they have learned to navigate life in different cultures, in Delhi or Dubai or in London or Los Angeles. We left Kashmir as the storm clouds gathered, and we live now wanting to bring our heritage of experience of the 'then' and the 'now', to help the next generation find their way. In Birmingham, as in Srinagar, we have lived in a setting where people of differing faiths and cultures, especially Muslims, Christians and people of no religion, live in close contact, so the question of my minor key is, 'How can people of clear and distinct faith live faithfully and peacefully together in today's world?' As I muse on mountains and friends in these pages that is my minor key. For me, this book is a preface. I hope to start work soon on Life before and after Kashmir, in Britain as it was and in Birmingham as it now is. For now, the following pages, written at different times over the last sixty years, are simply a little slice of life as we knew it.

Welcome to that Happy Valley.

TAJIKISTAN

Wakhan

AFGHANISTAN

Mintaka Pass

Shaksgam Valley

Ceded by Pakistan to China. Contested by India

CHINA

Traditional boundary claimed by the former princely state of Jammu and Kashmir

Gilgit

K2

Aksai Chin

Indus

Nanga Parbat

Seized by China in 1962. Contested by India

Muzaffarabad

Wular Lake

Cease fire line of actual control

Kargil

Srinagar

Zojila Pass

Ladakh

Leh

Kashmir valley

Azad Kashmir

ISLAMABAD

Kashmir

Padum

Zanskar

Indus

Tibet (China)

Mirpur Tehsil whence 60% of British Pakistanis

Jammu

Jhelum

Chenab

P A K I S T A N

Lahore

Amritsar

Sutlej

Shimla

Punjab

N

0   100
km

I N D I A

NEPAL

New Delhi

XX

1
A GLIMPSE THROUGH THE CLOUDS

Coming from Pakistan that January morning in 1960, I was regarded with suspicion by my reluctant host in Amritsar, but next morning managed to get on the old Dakota for Srinagar. The plane struggled up to twelve thousand feet, looking down first on green wheat fields then on pine-clad hills. Beyond the deep trench of the Chenab the tiny terraced fields and flat-roofed *gujar* huts were snow-covered, and as the high mountains came into view I asked if I could go to the front. Ahead was the Banihal pass, a dip in the circle of peaks which ringed the Valley of Kashmir, frozen and invisible under its winter cloud blanket. One looked out on a saw-edged saucer full of milk. The serrated pinnacles and the upper face of the cloud were bright in sunlight. Far ahead, due north, Nanga Parbat stood guard over the old Gilgit Agency, now ruled by Pakistan. Soon the plane dipped into the cloud, down and down for an uncomfortable length of time. Then suddenly we were scurrying close above almond gardens on a dry, snow-skiffed plateau. The airfield fence rushed up to meet us across a ravine; we bumped and landed.

Passengers were few, and I was the sole tourist. The Indian Airlines bus took us past bare wintry poplars, fields and houses. A grubby bazaar led up to the bridge over the River Jhelum. On its bank stood one rather fine white building. This was the Old Palace, by then the home of the Legislative Assembly. Twenty years later, Catherine and I would walk down the *bund*, five minutes from our home, to stand on the bridge and watch the Palace burn. Along with the rest of the silent crowd that evening, we would wonder whether the fire was caused by an impending audit, by faulty wiring or in the hope of manipulating a reaction from government, knowing only that we would never know. The bus turned into the Tourist Centre, and as I stepped off with only a small rucksack I was engulfed by houseboat *wallas*. As the single prey, I was fair game. Having only a month earlier taken part with the boys in the Lawrence College cross country, I was in good trim, so took to my heels and ran. They ran after me laughing and shouting, and it was half way down the Polo Ground before they gave up.

Pausing to survey the scene, I was in an avenue of cathedral-like plane trees, the Kashmiri *chenars*. This was the old 'civil lines' area, of houses and shops in a somewhat English style. In a few minutes, past a small park, the road broadened out into Lal Chowk, or Red Square as I call it. To the right was the Bus Station, ahead was the *Chowk*, and to the left through a small gate in a crumbling fence, the Tyndale Biscoe School. The whole area, normally crowded and sometimes tumultuous, was quiet in winter gloom. Every Kashmiri who can leaves the Valley in winter. The peasant farmers leave their frozen fields to seek work in Delhi or the Punjab, while on the analogy of the King's Bench, the State Government still follows the practice of the Dogra Maharajahs who moved to Jammu as their winter capital. When the *Darbar* moved, so did the State Government, down to the humblest clerk. Their families moved with them. The law courts moved, so that if you were on the slippery slope towards losing a case in the Srinagar courts in October, you only had to delay a little, perhaps to pay the Court Clerk a small sum, and you could relax until May.

I paused at the entrance to this unique school where later my wife and I were to live for twenty-five years. On this occasion, it was closed, and I had been told that the staff touring club was in South India. I expected to see no-one but Miss Mallinson, an elderly missionary lady. I pushed open the gate and walked past closed buildings, across a paddock between *chenar* trees and was stopped in front of what looked like a small Tudor manor house by a head which came out of an upstairs window. 'Are you the man who's coming from Pakistan, marrying a doctor, and going to be Principal?' My mouth fell open making denial useless. The secret was out. I mumbled something and was directed to another crumbling manor, 'Miss Mallinson's', half visible behind two more giant *chenars*.

The lady I was about to meet had lived here in Sheikh Bagh for nearly forty years, being paddled down to the Girls' School in the Old City, under five of the nine bridges each day by her faithful servant and boatman, Sultana. Some of her girls became her teachers, almost the first literate Muslim women in the City. Canon Biscoe had said, 'I cannot do any more for the boys in Kashmir until someone does something for the girls', and she had gone, and had stayed. Now she was ready to retire, but there was no-one to take over. Her landlords wanted to take back her School; other schools now had graduate teachers, while she still had matriculates.

Like the gentleman who had stuck his head out of the window opposite, she had heard of Catherine and me (we were engaged at the time) from Jenny Lane, an Englishwoman who had knocked about the North West Frontier for many years. Jenny, who kept a houseboat up the river for the summers, had met us, knew of our hopes, and had written to Chandra Pandit, so the secret was out. Muriel Mallinson greeted me with caution—I came from

Pakistan—but said I should stay the night and meet some of the staff, and Mr Salamuddin, the Vice Principal. The road was blocked by snow and stone falls, and the staff touring club had not yet been able to get out of Kashmir.

It was immediately clear that Kashmir was somehow different from any other place I had been in. The climate, the style of building, the language, the way people communicated by gesture, silence or glance. Fairly quickly I felt not excluded, but somehow a child among a circle of adults. The Valley would not quickly share its hidden history. However, this was in the future. The night was freezing hard and the bed had not been warmed. In the morning Muriel took me over to the School. Smoke poured out of a stovepipe; the *bukhari* had been lit, and a dozen or so men were gathered around it. Introductions made, I soon found myself being thoroughly quizzed. The standard of English was good, the rapport and humour among the group was strong, their frequent lapses into Kashmiri impenetrable. They learned a lot about me, I very little about them. They seemed to like me, to want me to come. With hindsight it was clear that whatever a bishop in Amritsar (we were a diocesan school) or a society in London might think, this was effectively my job interview. Should this group of men not want me, a quiet word with a relation in intelligence would be quite sufficient. Word came that the road might open next day, so attention was diverted. 'Hope to see you in about two years,' they said, as Mr Salamuddin led me through Maisuma, and over Amirakadal (First Bridge) to his home beside a small Central Asian style mosque.

Pir Salamuddin, whose green turban proclaimed his spiritual standing, was a man of quiet wisdom with entrée to most households in the City. Slight in build and quick in movement, he would be my Number Two. In the meantime, he began to teach me. Sitting cross legged on a crewel-stitch rug, a blanket over my knees and a *kangri* to warm me, we looked out of open wooden shutters on the scene below. *Kahvah*, sweet spiced green tea, was brought, and then rice with *goguj* (turnip) and *sag* in a hot curry. Eat with the right fingers only, up to the first knuckle. It was soon clear that neither church and diocese, nor mosque, saw any conflict in *Pir* Sahib's roles. Was I a trained teacher? Did I know about the school camps in the mountains, the annual swim across the Dal Lake, the weekly regattas, the Mahadev climb?

The next day I flew out.

2
THE DELECTABLE VALLEY

This passage was written soon after we left Kashmir in 1986, before the massive increase in unplanned development that has so harmed the beauty of the land, and when there were far fewer direct flights from Delhi. Beauty and peace are still to be found, but much further back from the main highway. Then most visitors arrived by bus, or perhaps taking a seat in a taxi from Jammu. Now far more travel by air.

So many thousands will remember their entry into the Kashmir Valley. The bus from Jammu has toiled for six or eight hours, or maybe in the case of landslide for two or more days. It has been halted by convoys, civil or military, has lurched steeply up and down, round innumerable bends, poised over crumbling precipices, its passengers drinking deeply of diesel fumes. At last the tributary streams of the mighty Chenab River have been left behind and the road has climbed again to over seven thousand feet before disappearing into the tunnel, built by German engineers in the fifties, under the Banihal Pass. Then light appears and soon the Kashmir Valley is laid out below. Mostly the drivers hurry on to their destination, to the city forty-six miles distant, but my notional bus comes to a halt looking out over what appears as a great plain rather than a valley.

On all sides, fading to the far distance, are mountains, snow-capped for all but the brief summer months. Below the high mountains comes a shelf, widest on the Pir Panjal slopes to the west, of forest. Below the forests is another belt, this time of dissected dry plateau, fissured with streams wide or small. The plateaux or *karevas* are cultivated with almond orchards, or with maize, apples or saffron. The higher Kashmiri villages are mainly hidden among trees near the streams which carry the snowmelt down to the Valley floor. This is the heart of Kashmir, a broad open area of irrigated land, where the staple crop is rice. Only in a few parts of the world does the rice harvest depend on the previous winter's snowfall, melting steadily from the snowfields and glaciers above.

This lowest broad strip of the Valley, here and there interspersed with dry fingers of *kareva*, centres on the River Jhelum. Though the smallest of the Five Rivers, the *Panch Ab* or Punjab as the land of the Five Rivers is named, the Jhelum is the historic artery of Kashmir. It was, until the coming of modern roads, the main highway for traffic. The Jhelum rises in part from springs gushing out at Verinag, close below the Banihal Pass. Tributaries, such as the sparkling Lidder or the Sindh from the east, add to it as it meanders down, increasingly muddy as it goes along, passing under the nine bridges of Srinagar. Flowing north-west, and then west through the now diminished Wular Lake, the river passes out of the Valley beyond Baramulla. A great gorge carries it rushing down from the Valley floor at 5,200 feet to Kohala at 1,900 feet above the far distant sea level. Geologists say that the Kashmir Valley is in fact a series of levels of earlier lake floor, the level of outflow falling as the ice which had dammed the exit from the Valley retreated.

The colours changing with the seasons, it is the rice fields and villages which stretch the seventy miles from Qazigund below the Banihal to Baramulla that most typify 'Kashmir'. Seen from above, the land is punctuated by dark masses, by groups of the huge *chenar* trees, each as broad as it is high. These commonly dwarf the sheltering villages, though they also stand as massive sentinels beside the roads or elsewhere. The landscape is almost defined by trees: the long lines of pencil poplars, willows along the streams, mulberries hacked to ugliness to feed silkworms.

Entering a village, there are more trees around its large thatched or metal sheet roofed houses. Perhaps because of its value as a cash crop, the walnut is usually close to the houses. Every part of each tree has its use; for shade, for feed for the sheep, or to burn as charcoal in the *kangri*. Even the green husks of the walnut are rotted and pressed for use as a stain.

The Banihal Road has been the only widely used route into Kashmir since 1947, but prior to that the main entry was from the railhead at Rawalpindi, up through Murree to enter the State by Kohala bridge, and so up the Jhelum gorge from Muzaffarabad into the Valley at Baramulla. This was 'Spedding's Road', built between 1880 and 1892, when the Maharajah was driven to Domel in a bullock cart. Well-engineered and graded, it revolutionised the economy of the Valley. The cease-fire line established in 1949 closed this road at Uri, some miles below Baramulla.

Otherwise there is the tortuous summer route over the Zoji La to Ladakh, and indeed on from Leh to Manali over the Rohtang. There is also a road (if it has been completed) by which I walked into the State in 1982, using the route from Chamba in Himachal to Bhadawah. The other ancient routes are all closed by unfriendly frontiers. For all practical purposes 'the road' is the former Maharajah's Road, opened for him to drive up in his Rolls Royce, accompanied by his vast entourage each May, after great gangs of coolies had cleared (for a short while) the landslides and rock falls. Built with disregard for strata and seepage, it still plagues the engineers who maintain it.

In many ways the most attractive parts of the Valley are the approaches to the mountains, side valleys and villages off the beaten track. Even by 1986 when we left these were being pressed back year by year, but they will still survive. The tumbling streams, the myriad wild flowers and birds, and the life of the countryside will just have retreated a little further.

Part of the fascination of Kashmir is its sheer difference from anywhere else. For most of history it has been sealed off by remoteness. Its language, descended from Pali, the source of Sanskrit, is incomprehensible to Punjabis, and even to the Mirpuris and other peoples of what Pakistanis now call 'Azad' Kashmir. The strongest weapon of the Kashmiri may be his or her humour. Long inured to fear and injustice, he keeps his views to himself and studies how to placate or please his master of the moment.

It is an area of great variety, in landscape, in its people and its history. Turning off the Baramulla Road ten miles from Srinagar, one passes through the usual rice fields, then up a dry track on to a *kareva*. Without any care or even a notice board there stand extensive ruins, great blocks of stone, the remains of Parisapura, capital city of Lalitaditya (reigned 699 to 735). There are many remains everywhere of a rich and settled kingdom, of ancient canals, temples and palaces. Most of these ruins stand apart from habitation on *karevas*, isolated and silent, looking to the snows of Haramukh. The *pheron*-clad goatherd knows nothing of the ancient culture of Kashmir.

The human factor, as always, adds a deeper resonance to the natural scene. The willows overhang the stream, the hills beyond reflected in its waters, but it is the shepherd who feeds his sheep on the leaves who somehow completes the picture. In the modern urban world speed and anonymity rob us of our humanity. In the Kashmir villages the life of the community is plain for all to see. Children play, tethered farm animals look out from the yards, winter supplies are collected and stored in the large open lofts. Arguments are prolonged public displays of verbal intensity. The whole web of rural culture has come down from time immemorial. It is no halcyon picture, human nature being what it is. Village women in the extremities of labour have been known to refuse the keys of their tin trunks to their nearest relatives. But it is, or was until recently, a society of detailed regulation, of *dastur*—iron-bound tradition, of known boundaries.

The Banihal Pass is the lowest point of the Pir Panjal range. This outer rim of the high Himalaya guards the south-west and western fringes of the Valley, and swings round in a wide arc as far as Baramulla. Beautiful deep gorges lead up to mountain lakes such as Konsarnag, and above the tree line are wide grassy expanses, grazed by flocks of sheep and goats in summer. The highest peaks are Tatakuti and Sunset Peak at 15,555 and 15,560 feet. It is said that on a clear day the glass roof of Lahore railway station can be seen from the latter summit, but on my visit the mists were rolling in, and we saw nothing. These mountains are Indian held, the cease-fire line being to the west.

In much of the Himalaya the mountains are remote and difficult to reach, but in Kashmir, rather as in the Austrian Alps, the approach is gradual. There is a symbiosis between the mountains and the City as well as the villages, in matters such as knowledge of the medicinal plants found at different altitudes. At the request of an elderly *Pandit* I promised to look for a rare plant, a Yog Badshah, from a cleft at 15,000 feet on Tatakuti. This cauliflower-like plant, as Mr Radhakrishen Kaul told me on my successful return, would heal those sicknesses for which no other cure sufficed.

As always, the approaches to the mountains have their own delights. The pines, retreating and at first lopped of most of their branches, grow denser as open glades of roses and banks of wild strawberries alternate with stands of deodar, pine and spruce. In summer the scent of the pines adds fragrance to the silence. Then at about ten thousand feet the conifers begin to give way to birch and juniper and then to the *margs* or meadows, summer pastures briefly peopled by Kashmiri shepherds and nomadic *bakarwals*. Beyond this was my kingdom of delight, the untouched world of the mountains.

Of that, more later!

3
A REMARKABLE SCHOOL

It was Dr Phil Edmonds, Principal of the Biscoe School from 1947 to 1954, who first suggested that I consider applying for the post of Principal of the Srinagar School as the Bishop of Amritsar, Chairman of Governors, was seeking someone suitable from the UK. He warned me not to get too close to political leaders in Kashmir. Phil had been friendly with Sheikh Abdullah and had co-operated with him in the foundation of the Kashmir University. When in 1953 Sheikh Sahib had been removed from power and imprisoned, Dr Edmonds became suspect and had to leave India. He went to Pakistan and improved Edwardes College Peshawar so greatly that by local demand it alone among Christian colleges escaped nationalisation under Bhutto in 1975. It still flourishes amid the storms in the Peshawar of the twenty-first century.

Phil's advice was good but hard to follow. On arriving in Srinagar, I found that the heads of nine government departments were Old Boys. Six out of seven Chief Ministers in the succeeding twenty-five years were either Old Boys or parents of children in the School, or both. More than this, their wives in several cases were Old Girls of Miss Mallinson's School. Given that many of our teachers, who were often private tutors in ministers' homes, were also former students and that everyone, it seemed, wanted admission, the position of Principal of the Biscoe School was one of some influence. This could be uncomfortable, as when Mr Sadiq, Chief Minister in 1965, rebuked me in front of three thousand people for planning to demolish Canon Biscoe's house, calling it the house of the founder of modern Kashmir. Unfortunately, by 1962 it was a rotting rat-infested barn. I was to learn how this one school had such an influence on the development of society.

As Principal of the School I also had a unique window on the world of Kashmir where we were privileged to gain some insight into the minds and hearts of its peoples.

And what a school it was! Cecil Earl Tyndale Biscoe came from a landed family which included an admiral and a general. Cox of the Cambridge boat in 1882, his nose broken twice while boxing at school, converted under Moody's preaching at Cambridge; in his culture he was an unreconstructed imperialist. But he loved the Kashmiris and the Kashmiris loved him, perhaps in part because he shared their sense of humour. This excerpt from his *Kashmir in Sunlight and Shade* explains why.

On a country road leading up a short, steep hill I overtook a party of fourteen coolies carrying sacks of grain on their backs. They were evidently very tired, for they were groaning as they trudged along, it was towards evening and they had been at this hard labour all day. So, I went up to one of them who was an undersized man who seemed to be more fagged than the rest and asked him if he was tired. He said, 'Yes, very tired and ready to die, if not already dead.' I told him to get on my back, as I would carry him on my back up the hill. He stared at me, opening his mouth and eyes wide and shook his head. However, I insisted, and made him get on my back with his load, for I was then young and fit. I carried him to the top of the hill and then deposited him and his load, whereupon the whole gang, who had trudged up the hill with me, put their loads on their cross-bar sticks behind, placed their legs apart and roared and roared with laughter, and when they had recovered their wind started off again, laughing loudly, and continued to do so till out of hearing, their tiredness forgotten.

The grounds we occupied, Sheikh Bagh or 'The King's Garden', had been granted by the Maharajah to CMS in the 1880s. As in so many Indian cities 'The Mission' was set between the 'civil lines' area where officials, British residents and visitors lived, and the old City. Over many years Biscoe had developed a network of primary schools, with the Central High School set high above the River Jhelum at Fateh Kadal. Sheikh Bagh, with its majestic *chenar* trees, housed Mr Biscoe's House, the Ladies Mission House and Barton House. In time a primary school was built there, and in 1910 a hostel for boys from Gilgit and Ladakh. When in 1937 our Pastor Yonathan set off from his home at Shey in Ladakh it was a sixteen-day walk to School. The same year a new secondary school, which later became the Tyndale Biscoe School, was built. Twelve years later the Central High School was handed to its teaching staff and the branch schools were disposed of.

After Dr Edmunds left in 1954, acting Principals came and went in quick succession, and the School became an orphan, its fences broken and hope declining. The large under-used area of invaluable ground with its paddocks and gardens, set in the growing commercial area of the City, awaited development. I remember a sense of surprise that no-one had seized it, and a dawning realisation that the reputation and status of the School was such as to make this impossible. There was thus a great need to develop the grounds properly, though no funding to do so.

In 1960 Eric Tyndale Biscoe and his wife Phil had come back from retirement in New Zealand to lead the School until someone permanent could be found. By then it was managed by the Anglican Diocese of Amritsar, which had been split off from Lahore Diocese following Partition in 1947. Bishop Kenneth Anand, lacking Indian Christians with a background which would fit them for the headship of such a school in Kashmir, had approached CMS in London. Catherine and I offered to the Society long service in this school, and thus it was that in January 1962 we arrived with all our worldly belongings in Radha Krishan's mail bus. It had taken two days from the railhead, which was then at Pathankot, 240 mountain miles distant. Phil and Eric welcomed us into their home, and some of the teachers I had briefly met two years earlier were there to greet us.

Until the Biscoes left in July we shared with them what had become a ramshackle old house. The old regime still operated, with a cook, a *bearer*,[2] a *sweeper* and a *mali* each doing their own prescribed work, besides the *chuprassi* who ran errands and collected post. We made mental notes that the system was overdue for change. It left one with little privacy, not that much was possible anyway. Mr Salamuddin, Vice Principal, asked me to be careful what I put in letters home, as 'some of the masters' had not appreciated my comments. Quite apart from at least two official censorships, by the Central and the State Governments, everyone else clearly wanted to know our thoughts. Letters thus became innocuous.

Eric Biscoe had for many years served as Vice Principal to his father and, as well as rebuilding fences and walls, was seeking to revive traditions of the School which had become neglected. It was valuable to see the old system re-erected,

---

2 Italicised terms are explained in the Glossary, see pp. 154-7.

whether or not we would keep it unchanged. Biscoe had taught his boys to swim to save life in days when most traffic was by river, canal or lake. This was wonderful, but I was somewhat suspicious when a master who seemed to me something of a flatterer recommended the un-athletic son of the Director of Education for a life-saving award on the Honours Board. Kindness to animals, in a society where this was notably lacking, had been another aspect of Biscoe's School. The rusting Dog Ambulance was repaired, and mangy dogs were duly presented for treatment. Times had changed. But the stray dogs who so largely consumed scraps from the boys' meals, and in turn fouled the School grounds, thus, perhaps, needed the alternative treatment of the municipal dog warden.

As well as receiving great kindness from Eric and Phil, we also learned much from them. The rotting school *shikaras* had been replaced or repaired and weekly regattas on the still largely unpolluted Dal Lake restored. The swimming pool was repaired and the Poor Fund re-invigorated. New vigour was given to the wonderful yearly round of activities. Beyond all this we were given a glimpse of an earlier age, and were introduced to Eric and Phil's friends, people from varied faiths and from every social class. Especially I remember the retired teachers, nearly all Kashmiri *Pandits*. These were Old Boys of Canon Tyndale Biscoe, some of whom had broken tradition at his behest. One, Shanker Koul, former Headmaster, was, we were told, the first Kashmiri Brahmin to marry a widow. Prior to this, in days of child marriage and of frequent child deaths in epidemics, child widows had been condemned to virtual slavery or prostitution in the homes of their dead child husbands. Men like Shanker, or like Samsar Chand Kaul the naturalist, had somehow combined exposure to Biscoe's vigorous style of education with lives still lived within the complex Brahmin traditional world of old Srinagar. After 1947, when Dr Edmonds had concentrated work in the one School, only the most able staff were continued. These Dr Edmonds helped and trained by example and were the core of the staff I was fortunate to inherit. The best of them, all Old Boys, and all except Mr Salamuddin, *Pandits*, would have graced any school anywhere by their ability, devotion and identification with the School. How otherwise, over a period of twenty-five years, could I have led the School successfully? It was a team effort.

The Round of the Year in the Biscoe School

The School year began in March with the mass cross-country run from the School to the top of Takht-i-Suleiman. The route lay along the riverside *bund* beside the Jhelum, past Suffering Moses' Handicrafts shop and the savage-looking stuffed bear outside the furriers, then dodging under the smelly egrets' nesting colony in the *chenar* trees beside the old British Residency, now an Arts Emporium. Past All Saints Church the boys began to straggle up by the hill foot cemetery where bones could be seen sticking out as the bank fell away. Climbing the steep and stony track, the Valley and the Pir Panjal mountains came into view. Below was the Dal Lake with its lines of houseboats, and Akbar's Fort on Hari Parbat Hill beyond. The first green of the willows and the faint pink blossom in the almond gardens lent colour to an often dark and rainy sky. The Ladakhi boys moved ahead up the track. With lungs developed at 12.000 feet, they had an advantage, and usually won the race. Staff gave out different coloured tickets at different points for the runners to prove that they had not taken a short cut. After reaching Shankracharya Temple at the top, a helter-skelter downhill run followed with some nasty tumbles but never a broken bone. Back to the School playing field, the winning time was about 45 minutes. Everyone who completed the run gained house points and had memories of a testing run.

'Regatta' started weekly from 1 May, with some twenty racing *shikaras*, twelve boys to each. There was much noise and enthusiasm as they all changed, piled into boats at the Dal Gate boatshed, and paddled up to the narrows at Nehru Park. The four Houses, named after Kashmir mountains: Kolahoi, Haramukh, Tatakuti and Mahadev, each had four boats in house colours. Those not racing cheered from the bank. Most entertaining was the Sinking Race. As the boats sped along, at the given signal from the Principal, their crews stood up and ran over the front into the water. They then turned the boats, 'bottoms up' and re-floated them. While crew members held up the boats in the water or swam around collecting paddles, one boy clambered in and began splashing out. Then another climbed in, and so on till the whole crew were seated, all the water expelled, and they raced on to the finishing point. Sometimes they started up too quickly with water still in the boat, and sank again, to repeat the process and trail wearily in at the end. As with most of Biscoe's innovations, there was a purpose. In this case it was that boys should not be frightened, and should know what to do, if they were in a boat which sank.

The tenth class of about 120 boys, with a good number of staff, climbed Mahadev each year over the first weekend in June. On the Thursday after school we squeezed into buses to Harwan, passing Nishat and Shalamar gardens on the way. From the road end we would struggle up in parties of ten, with our personal kit and with heavy bell tents, bags of rice and utensils, to camp among the cherry orchards of Dara. In the early morning tea and *chapatis* were made as the sun lit the snows to the west, and the Valley stirred into life. A line of porters, led by Ali Mohammed, came around the hillside to take the heavy loads, while the boys carried their own belongings. The porters were not Kashmiris but Pathans who had settled generations before around the fringes of the Valley. Our route lay up the Mahadev Nallah, past cherry orchards and a little water mill into a gorge, sometimes high above the stream, then descending to cross it. Some years the water was high, and a rope would safeguard the boys across. At one place we crossed by a giant fallen tree. We would pass and be passed by a variety of people. There were *gujars*, moving up with their flocks to summer pastures, women with babies, blankets and utensils on ponies, or villagers carrying firewood. We struggled up to Lidwas to camp at the highest huts, not yet occupied after the winter. Tents were pitched on the flat roofs, the only level ground. We were among the last of the trees at nearly 11,000 feet, among birch and rhododendron, and the last sentinel conifers. Primulas and gentians were among the flowers peeping out beside the streams where the snowbeds had just retreated. Boys slumped asleep then stirred to collect firewood. Cooking was shared between boys and masters, Hindu and Muslim.

Next day the pattern was repeated. The long line moved slowly up across boulder and then snow fields to a col. A small party of enthusiasts, with rope and ice axe, would move off to a *gulley* while the long crocodile wound round ridges, up little walls and then one last longer ridge, steep but easy, to the top. We looked down on a marvellous panorama from over 13,000 feet. The City lay in haze, but Akbar's fort at Hari Parbat stood out, and, far beyond, the whole snowy range of the Pir Panjal. We could see the Valley of Kashmir from end to end. We lazed in the sun, exchanged mangoes or other delicacies, and finally roused ourselves for the long descent. From the col the snow stretched down, in a good year, for a thousand feet. Steep at the top, this made for a marvellous glissade. Tiredness forgotten, small figures climbed up again and again. Back at camp the parties, sharing with teachers and porters, made ready to cook, and prepared songs and small camp fire 'dramas'. At repeated request, Ali Mohammed and some of his porters would add their wild and whirling *Khattak* dance, applauded by the circle of fire-lit faces under the stars.

The following day we walked down into the Valley's midday heat to find the buses waiting for us under the chestnut gardens of Harwan for the journey back round the Dal Lake.

But it was the 'Dal Cross' which was the big event of the year. Held on the first Saturday of July, the three-and-a-half-mile swim, or seven miles for those who re-crossed, was by far our most dangerous activity. In many Srinagar homes the framed Dal Cross certificate held pride of place beside the graduation one. In the seventies the School was still paying pensions to the widows of six teachers who had been drowned when overtaken by a storm in the Wular Lake in 1935, but thankfully we never lost a boy on the Dal. Preparation was thorough. First, all those in each House who had swum two lengths of the swimming pool swam 'round the boats'. All twenty school boats were tied in a long line, crewed by previous 'Dal Crossers', and the new swimmers swam three circuits of the line, clambering on to a boat if they needed to give up. The next week was the 'One Mile Swim' from the steps near the Maharajah's summerhouse back to Nehru Park. Again, the previous year's Dal Crossers manned the fleet of escorting *shikaras*, ready to pull out an exhausted swimmer. Then came the big swim.

The day before we had gone across the route looking for dangerous weed patches and planting a line of flagpoles leading to the finish at Nishat Bridge. Early in the morning boys arrived walking, on cycles or by car. The swimmers oiled their bodies and were counted and checked by housemasters. We watched the sky anxiously, hoping for a dull day without wind. All the School *shikaras*, and about thirty hired ones, were marshalled to the right of the long lines of boys. At 8.50 am the first of the juniors entered the water. Within five minutes the Middle School were going in, then by 9 o'clock the seniors. As the line lengthened with about 250 boys swimming, the escorting *shikaras*, one by one, kept pace. Three *shikaras*, each with a senior teacher and four men paddling, began making continuous circuits to monitor and correct distances between escorts. In spite of care it was easy for a large gap to develop. On the steps at the one mile narrows each swimmer called out his number as he swam past and continued into the open Lake. We settled into a watchful routine. The medical *shikara*, with the school nurse or doctor, stayed near the middle of the line. Boys became hungry, and staff in the three circling *shikaras* opened large sacks of *kulchas*, Kashmiri 'breads', to toss them across to the raised arms of swimmers calling 'kulcha, Sir!' A *dunga*, meantime, was being poled across the lake carrying the named bundles of the swimmers' clothing. It also carried large degs, cooking pots, full of curry, a meal for swimmers on arrival and for escorts.

The dunga halted beside the finish, an arched Moghal bridge on the causeway, half a mile from Nishat. A fringe of willows gave shade as swimmers came to the finish, each number being checked off. Escorting boys, and masters in their *shikaras*, were given their meals and sometimes needed to be urged to get back on the Lake, as those still swimming began to 're-cross'. We allowed 're-crossers' to start back until 1pm. Some years as many as two hundred boys, some of them juniors, completed the crossing, and fifty or more set off on the re-cross. The afternoon wore on in drowsy July heat. The swimmers were fewer but more widely scattered, and tiring. One by one, a few gave up. Back at Nehru Park those watching waited to see the first heads bobbing in the water, and, so slowly, moving towards the shore. Some parents would be present, proud of their son's feat. It was not a race, but a loud cheer always greeted the first 're-crossers' to arrive. After six or more hours in the water they felt so heavy that they could hardly climb out. Others got into the water to help them up the steps to lie on the warm stone while a blanket was wrapped round them and a cup of *kahava*, Kashmiri green tea, brought to their lips. The fairer skinned, and especially albinos, suffered sunburn. So slowly the last few swimmers doggedly continued, each with an escort. The last to land usually got a bigger cheer than the first. Towels and blankets and belongings were collected, and anyone who lacked transport taken back to School. One more Dal Cross Day was over.

The approach to the mountains is especially beautiful and full of interest in Kashmir. Elsewhere in the Himalaya huge gorges bar the way to the high peaks, but the mountains around the Kashmir Valley are on a human scale, somewhat like the Austrian Alps. The side valleys, with their fast-flowing rivers, and with groves of walnut and *chenar* concealing the villages from view, are full of interest. Kashmiris mingle with *gujars* and *bakarwals*. The sixties and seventies were by and large a peaceful and prosperous time, Sheikh Abdullah's reforms having given land to the villagers. As well as rice, watered by snow-melt from mountain streams, there is wheat on the drier ground and maize on the hillside terraces. Apples, honey, saffron and almonds are among the cash crops. Nothing is wasted. The leaves of every tree have their uses, whether the willow or acacia, as fodder for the sheep kept by villagers, or as fuel, like the charcoal made from *chenar* leaves.

This marvellous countryside would be explored each week by a 'class expedition'. Typically, a group of thirty boys would reach School by 7.30 am, climb into the back of a country bus and set off for some point in a side valley. Keeping a steady pace into the high forests the party would climb to a pass, pause for a bite of food and descend into some distant and, to them, unknown side glen to reach and ford a stream. We would open *tiffin carriers* under the shade of the willows beside the river, then move on, often more slowly in afternoon heat, to find a bus waiting at some village terminus to carry us, as well as the villagers, back to the City.

By the end of June, Summer Camp, a week for Middle School and a week for Seniors, was being planned. We had a four-year rotation of sites, choosing as our base places in the mountains accessible by bus. Sonamarg was to the north-east, on the road to Ladakh, Pahlgam to the south-east, Yusmarg on the edge of the Pir Panjal to the south-west, and Gulmarg to the west. At each place we also set up 'high camp', some ten or more miles further in, and three or four thousand feet higher. Boys would be asked to bring 'rations' of rice, *atta* and sugar, also blankets and money. The Advance Party left with truckloads of tents and supplies. They would set up camp and arrange with local hill men for ponies, then move up to establish high camp in some remote and beautiful place.

High Camp was an experience of the mountains which surely left its mark on many children. Pitched beside a rushing river, far above the tree-line in a setting of grandeur, the long line of weary boys would arrive in sunshine or storm, while the cooks fought with the elements and the smoky juniper roots to make tea and then supper. Middle School boys came for one night, next morning returning to the main camp and passing the party coming up. The Seniors stayed for two nights. In the intervening day the main party would trek to some mountain lake, while the enthusiasts climbed a peak, perhaps at fourteen or fifteen thousand feet. There were so many good days of adventure together, unforgotten experiences of fun and of beauty among the high flowery valleys with their straths and deep silent rivers, the snowfields above leading across cols to awe-inspiring views of distant ranges. If an educational theorist asked for the rationale of such effort, one would have to say in the end that 'the mountains are beautiful, and the adventure is life'. Kashmiri parents, most of them not wealthy, willingly paid the costs, and the boys and masters mostly joined in gladly. It all built up a strong camaraderie and pride in the School. Our parties travelling in the mountains were Kurt Hahn's 'little platoon' all over again.

Back at the main camp there were days in the forest or on steep ridges, back for tea and then games on the meadow. We ran the house volleyball finals, and sometimes played matches with a local police or military unit. At most campsites there was ample fallen timber, and a huge bonfire was built for the final night. After a special meal, usually attended by several parents who had driven up from Srinagar, the 'campfire' began. The songs and 'dramas' were greeted with enthusiasm by the circle of two or three hundred boys, sitting round in the firelight under the peaks above and the starry or moonlit sky. There was often an element of pure magic about it all, an enchantment of place, especially felt in a setting like the Glacier Valley at Thajiwas near Sonamarg.

Then followed two weeks of summer holidays, by the end of which the steamy heat of Srinagar in summer was beginning to pass. Autumn is a lovely season in Kashmir, with a long succession of clear warm days and increasingly crisp nights, with harvests of fruit and of rice, of walnuts and lastly of saffron, as the villagers laid in firewood and charcoal for their *kangris* for winter. By mid-September even the weekly class excursions gave way to preparation for the annual jamboree of 'Parents' Day', and then to thoughts of end of year examinations. There remained a great day on Zaberwan, the Twin Peaks, or a round of the whole circuit. By November nights were frosty and days cold. The last tourists, foreign and Indian, came and left by *Dussehra*. The State Government moved to Jammu, and Srinagar settled into its winter isolation.

During my time there was no ski lift to Khillan and beyond; only, by the time we left, a small tow from the Gulmarg Club up to near the hotel. Now, of course, the School year includes ski courses for the young. They, as well as tourists from far and wide, can be lifted without effort to over 13,000 feet. But in those times was not the effort part of the game?

4
KASHMIR REVISITED 2012

Having lived so long in Srinagar, Catherine and I were intrigued to receive an invitation in September 2012 to be guests at the Centenary Celebrations of the Mallinson Girls' School there. The School had marked the start of women's education in the State. Catherine was to be one of the chief guests. As well as being Principal of the Tyndale Biscoe School I had been the sister school's manager, and Catherine had run its Lower Primary Department for five years. We had both been deeply meshed in with local people at many levels, as also with All Saints, the local Protestant church.

Now for twenty-six years we had lived in Birmingham, deeply engaged in education as governors in local schools where the children are now mainly British Pakistanis from Mirpur District, in local charities and in our remarkable parish church, St Christopher's. Catherine had also worked as a doctor in a practice where many of the Pakistani-Mirpuri ladies spoke little or no English.

In March 2005 we had paid a visit to friends in North India and Kashmir. Among my files was one headed 'sad letters from Kashmir', received from both Kashmiri *Pandit* and Muslim friends in the intervening period. It included one from Professor Mohammed Ishaq Khan, from Srinagar in 1991 sent from 'this city of dreadful death'. Otherwise Kashmir seemed a closed book I was not expecting to re-open at the age of eighty-four. Then Parvez Samuel Kaul, my successor as Principal, announced that he was sending tickets, all expenses covered. The temptation was too much, and we began to pack again.

What would we find? India, as we had glimpsed in 2005, was developing at breakneck speed with huge new wealth but equally with continuing massive poverty. Kashmir had in 1989 descended into bloodshed as open revolt among many of the frustrated young, encouraged and armed from Pakistan and by a deepening Islamic radicalism, led to the flight of almost the entire Kashmiri *Pandit* (Brahmin) community after a succession of murders. Over twenty of our best teachers had gone in a single day, refugees in their own country. Our School was the leading City high school, but we also had a hostel for boys from Ladakh and Zangskar, the mainly Buddhist area of the State adjoining Tibet. Just before leaving a message came: 'The Old Boys here want you to come to Leh.' This sounded like the icing on the cake. We, our children and even grandchildren, have visited Ladakh over the years, building on friendships from the past. Chewang Motup of Rimo Travels, Old Boy and leading Himalayan travel guide, not only masterminded our stay in Leh but had us met and shepherded through airports throughout the trip, removing every worry. Everywhere we would be staying with friends, sharing some of their joys and sorrows over the years. The visit would be in three parts: prologue and finale in Delhi, main course in Srinagar, counterpoint to Muslim Kashmir in Ladakh. It goes without saying that our School in those (usually!) peaceful times had been no ordinary high school. As well as boating and long swims we introduced our boys to high mountains. If one shares repeated mountain adventure with boys there is a basis for lifelong relationship.

Delhi

Chewang's assistant met us at the Indira Gandhi International Airport and whisked us to 16 Pandit Pant Marg, the home of the Church of North India Synod, to be welcomed by its General Secretary Alwan Masih. Alwan had been a teacher on our staff around 1980. Our Chairman, Bishop Chandu Lal of Amritsar, had sent him to us and told me (more or less) to throw him into the Dal Lake and take him up a few mountains. The bishop saw us as training staff, as well as students, in adventure education enhancing leadership. Three years later the bishop took him away and sent him to Germany for youth work training. We next saw Alwan in 2005 as a top civil servant, in charge of personnel across India in the Ministry of Youth, Sport and Culture. Amazingly for a lad from a humble Punjabi family, he had been appointed by a minister in the BJP government, who said to him, 'Your religion is no business of mine. I have heard you are strictly honest: you will report direct to me.' Now seven years later he was at the heart of this Church of differing traditions, often thinly spread across the immense distances of India. A humble but decisive person, I guessed he would find the Church of North India just as challenging a field as the Government of India. Alwan, Nina and Rachel welcomed us into their simple flat, a gentle introduction to the teeming city of Delhi.

In 2005 we had seen something of the work of the Church among the very poor, and now we went again to the Delhi Brotherhood, a religious community of CNI, in its home outside Kashmiri Gate. We remembered the Night Shelter, where boys who earn a pittance on the streets helping at *chai* stalls or cleaning boots can bank their earnings, get a good supper and play simple games before sleeping safely. Many of them, including one now ordained priest, had arrived in Delhi as orphans, maybe on top of a train, to escape utter rural poverty. Those who show aptitude are helped into education and can stay in the hostel to study.

This time we were taken by Father Monodeep across East Delhi to the vocational training school where a whole variety of skills are taught. Boys were working at computers, at electrical and auto engineering. Girls were studying to be beauticians, also sewing and at computers. It was all simple and basic, but job related, and the lads assured us that they would be fitted for employment.

Returning through the crowded streets and *gulleys* of Old Delhi, sharing space with coolies pushing heavy carts, buffaloes and cows, rickshaws, people, cars and trucks, it all felt familiar. This was, of course, just an introduction to 'old' Delhi. Later we were to be astonished by the 'new'.

Kashmir

At the domestic airport there were far more flights to Kashmir than in days gone by. In the queue, mostly of Indians, one tall fair Kashmiri lady in *shalwar kamiz* stood out. Foreign tourists were still few, and she smilingly introduced herself as an Old Girl, now a bank manager. Knowing the family name, I asked about her brother. 'He was shot,' she replied, 'one of a crowd of students.'

So, we flew into that extraordinary valley ringed by mountain peaks. In the past one would look down on a mass of green rice fields, with small villages here and there hidden among huge *chenar* trees. Now there seemed fewer rice fields and the villages were much, much larger, sometimes almost meeting one another. Mr Kaul was at the airport to meet us. Everything was familiar: the gestures, the peculiar rather secretive look of many people. After all, it was home for twenty-five years. He took us round by the Indoor Stadium which he had booked for a Centenary event a week later.

It had been just being recovered for civil use after being requisitioned by the security forces for many years, and ours was the job of reclaiming it for civil society.

With no electricity or water, dirty, with rubbish and broken chairs everywhere, it looked impossible. But Mrs Joyce Kaul and forty school servants were on hand, thus perhaps there was hope.

So we came into Sheikh Bagh, the School grounds and a green oasis of quiet after school hours, through gates which announced 'No guns or ammunition beyond this point', as we left the crowds and traffic of Lal *Chowk* outside the walls. Parwez later explained that the notice was not for militants, who would hardly be dissuaded by such, but for self-important junior police officers or other would-be parents, vainly hoping to impress with their armed escorts.

For the next three weeks we were swept along on a tide of invitations, events and visits. We melded in to the Srinagar scene. The 'Tyndale Biscoe and Mallinson School Educational Society' in 2018 educates nearly eight thousand mainly middle-class children on five sites, and everyone gives Parwez (a state subject) and Joyce Kaul credit for sticking in Srinagar through the years of armed conflict and the very disturbed period that followed on and off up to 2010. Most schools were closed, but Sheikh Bagh had been open whenever possible despite fighting outside the gates. It was immediately apparent that the local atmosphere was now much relaxed. Soldiers were still to be seen and the newspapers reported shootings and bomb blasts in various parts of the Valley, but for the great majority life appeared normal. Trade was booming, and the tourist season had been excellent. Gangs of labourers were from Rajasthan or Bihar. Many Kashmiris were wealthy, sending remittances home from the Gulf or marketing handicrafts across India and beyond.

The Centenary Celebrations over three days were marked by enthusiasm and good presentations, with three government ministers attending, also the Chair of the Minorities Commission, Wajahat Habibullah. Bishop Samantaroy of Amritsar (our far-flung diocese) and other guests marked the wider Church's support. As a celebration of women's education much in the celebrations was very worthwhile. People remarked on the high standard of English, and Old Girls whom Catherine had taught now included medical specialists or lecturers. I was impressed by the work of the International Youth Award, the IYA, an Indian development from the Duke of Edinburgh's awards. Girls working towards the bronze, silver and gold awards and their mentors took the expedition, craft projects and service aspects very seriously. Dr Kurt Hahn, who had appointed me at Gordonstoun in 1953, would have been pleased as all this had been his inspiration.

It may be good to mention here, as a thread running through this book, the significance of Hahn's work. Before, during and since our time in Kashmir he has been my main educational inspiration. Springing from his experience of Germany during the period of cultural collapse which saw Hitler's rise to power, he developed methods and practices at Salem in Germany and Gordonstoun in Scotland aimed at making his schools 'islands of healing' in a sick society. Gordonstoun, situated between the mountains and the sea, was ideal for his purposes. Young people in small groups were trained and then sent out into the mountains or on the sea in small sailing ships. Such experience develops qualities such as initiative, loyalty, and courage. Hahn had great faith in the importance of the 'little platoon' as a nursery for all this, saying, 'There are no unbelievers in an open boat.' Seeing in modern society a threefold decay, of 'craftsmanship, of care and of compassion', he developed programmes which led on to the Duke of Edinburgh's award, seen in India today as the IYA. He had a strong belief in the willingness of the young to respond to requests for help and trained them for 'Samaritan service'. Today Gordonstoun has units of the Coastguard, Fire, and Mountain Rescue services. Parallels with Biscoe are quickly apparent. Looking at the educational scene today, in Britain or, I also suspect, internationally, dominant pressures reduce education to material success, sidelining the central importance of character.

Returning to Srinagar and the 2012 celebrations, I was delighted to find our Srinagar girls keenly involved in training for the International Youth Awards. The Indoor Stadium event with a capacity crowd of parents of both schools, was marked by enthusiasm and a fast moving and varied programme. It even included the girls dancing with exuberant freedom and a variety of musical and cultural items performed by both sexes: all this to the great applause of a large audience of local citizens. A senior magistrate, an Old Boy, commented to me that it would be hard work for the social and religious conservatives to put the clock back after this. Each day we interacted with a whole range of Srinagar folk. Sometimes in the street someone would recognise us from the past. Near Regal Chowk we were accosted by a handicraft seller who asked, 'Do you know Mr Ray?' to which the obvious reply was given. We were also privileged to have two informal meetings with Umar Abdullah, the then Chief Minister, as were his father and grandfather before him. However great the tensions and pressures of his situation, he hoped to do much for the people of Kashmir.

More widely, we observed contrary trends in Kashmir. A strong assertion of conservative religion seemed emphasised in the large number of new mosques, significantly often topped by an Arab dome, perhaps indicating Saudi Wahabi influence, rather than the traditional central Asian spire of Sufi-tending Kashmiri religion. But the burqa was not so common in Srinagar as in Birmingham, and there was little public sign of religious fervour. Pakistan was not even mentioned. More positively, it seemed to be beginning to be acceptable to ask questions. One of the many schools we visited, the Froebel Public School in Anantnag, impressed us in the quality of its head teacher and by its mission statement, showing three points of a triangle figuring a healthy body, a loving heart and an inquisitive mind. It states: 'In the Froebel Public School we will develop the full potential of our students in body, mind, heart and spirit. They will be the leaders of the future.' We were delighted also to see a very large new school, the Srinagar branch of Delhi Public School, which brings its pupils in over a hundred buses daily from all parts of the Valley, especially the villages to the south. Its Principal, our old student Vijay Dhar and his wife Kiran, left us in no doubt that for all the pressures of numbers and of finance, quality in education was their concern. Impossible pressures on admissions left no doubt of the need for more good schools.

So at least three forces may be discernible. Most obvious was the cascade of development and wealth with great numbers of grand new houses, dense urban traffic and sadly a level of pollution, in spite of government's best efforts, which will make the Valley a hell rather than a 'heaven on earth' if it cannot be checked and reversed. Second was a reassertion of conservative religion, perhaps with a radical fringe aimed at indoctrination of the young. Third is a dawning readiness to question received authority, an earnest searching for truth and reality. In the words of that fifteen-year-old already quoted, 'its renaissance!' Significantly two friends said, 'Since 9/11 many Muslims are studying Judaism, Buddhism and Christianity, especially the latter.' The internet was important in this search. 'Many,' they stressed, 'are thinking.'

Protestant and Roman Catholic schools remain among schools of choice. We visited two of them which had been burned following the threat by a maverick American preacher to burn the Quran. One, a new branch of the Biscoe School beside the forest at Tangmarg, was torched by the mob. Its headmaster, our Old Boy Rajinder Kaul, told me that his mobile phone was ringing till midnight, with children and parents weeping into the phone crying, 'Why have they burned our lovely school?' The Srinagar fire in St Paul's happened secretly at night. Both continued in temporary accommodation and have been rebuilt, the Tangmarg School with government assistance and the help of friends of the Biscoe Society.

Most public Christian work in the Muslim world is through medical or educational means. We stayed two nights in the former CMS hospital in Anantnag (Islamabad) a district town in the upper part of the Valley. It is a women's hospital which trains local girls as nurses and midwives and is in great demand. It is run with great dedication and professionalism by a team of about twenty-five workers led by Dr Sarah. They are mainly from Hyderabad in South India, members of the Laymen's Evangelical Fellowship of India.

We were repeatedly invited out to meet old students and others, made to feel welcome and, after so long a gap, part of the Srinagar family. Well organised and lively, often boisterous, occasions included a book launch, a meeting of the Mountaineering Club and an Old Students' dinner. Ones and twos of old students came to the door of our guest quarter late and early. It was a novel sensation for us to be VIP's! One always had to make a speech, and several times I found myself explaining how in 1962, as a young

Englishman only thirty-four years old, I had come to be Head of their famous school. My path had included five student years at St Andrews when mountains had been my passion, National Service in the Royal Marines and then teaching history and starting mountain training at Gordonstoun. It was, however, Andy's death climbing with me in Switzerland which had shaken me out of my comfort zone and strangely led me to northern Pakistan. There, as a lonely foreign teacher in the Lawrence College I had found meaningful Christian faith. Finding faith and thus God's purposes in life, and then meeting Catherine who was there to doctor in a Scottish Mission hospital, had led to the invitation to the Biscoe School.

Such gatherings enabled one to ask how far the disciplined and moral tone of the School, its Christian ethos, had helped or influenced them as Old Boys to 'make a difference' in society. The men I had known as teenagers were now senior government officers, professionals or businessmen. In a society deeply disfigured by corruption many of them were clearly excellent officers who worked for the common good by any means in their power. Their affection for us, and love for the School as they had known it, was very moving.

Days flew by and our regret is that we could not visit more friends in their homes. We did meet some of those few people, getting on in years but still active, whom we had been privileged to know as outstanding citizens.

Ladakh

On our plea that flying to Leh at 11,700 feet might be bad for my heart, Chewang had offered to send a car to Srinagar so that we could drive up in three easy stages. What a journey it was! The upper part of the Sindh Valley is still beautiful, the Zoji La still forbidding and grim. I recalled burying four tourists whose truck had hurtled over the edge thirty years ago: current unseasonal rain had made the road a chocolate coloured mudslide, but the driver was excellent. Then the ride into Ladakh steadily opens out into a magical moonscape, the choreographed rock forms, spires and gorges of a mountain desert with its precious shafts of cultivation wherever water trickles out. We stayed at a little guesthouse in the first mainly Buddhist village, Muhlbekh. The peace was almost tangible, sitting in the garden among hollyhocks and cosmos with the coloured mountains behind. Next day we luxuriated in the drive over the Namika la and the Foto la, then past the monastic fairyland of Lamayuru. Sonam our driver was phoning ahead and at the next village, Buzgo, we found out the reason.

A welcome party of ten, whom I remembered as boys but were now prominent citizens, were there in traditional dress to garland us with silk scarves and to accompany us to Leh where we had tea in the garden of the hotel that had been arranged for us. The next few days were quite wonderful. Our old hostel boys remembered the School as the 'best days of their lives' and wanted to say 'thank you'. Several of them made it clear that the 'extra' quality of our range of activities had been vital to their careers and some had a vision for doing good for society through their working lives. One at least, Phuntzog Kalon, whose family are leaders in the community, had long worked at grassroots level in co-operatives when he could have made money elsewhere. Another, Moses Kunzang, had just been appointed Commissioner for Ladakh, the highest civil office in the province.

Chewang himself, and his wife Yangdu, whose grandfather was Sherpa Tensing's brother, had hosted our son Ian on two expeditions to the Ladakh mountains. The previous year Ian's wife and three boys had climbed in

Nubra, and we found that their youngest, Jordan, then seven years old and with crampons, was something of a celebrity at 20.000 feet. Chewang and Yangdu have also visited us in Birmingham, and our elder daughter has visited old school friends in both Srinagar and Leh so we were almost family.

One of our oldest friends there is Rev Elijah Gergan, who was a boy in the School when we arrived in 1962. He is minister of the Moravian Church and grandson of Joseph Gergan, who translated the Bible into Tibetan. The Gergan family had been our close friends in Srinagar, Elijah's father being our daughter's godfather. We visited friends beside the Indus at Shey and in Leh. Chewang had wanted to take us up to Khardong, over the pass at 18,000 feet, but unseasonal snow closed the road. On our last night Mustafa hosted a party at his Grand Dragon Hotel where a splendid cultural group, musicians and dancers, so enthused us that everyone joined in the dance. In the morning the same party took us to the airport where even the security officer was an Old Boy. Our VIP treatment, with silk scarves and the front seats in the plane, must have left other passengers bemused. Leh had been a very special experience. Not only did we greatly enjoy the warmth and affection we met, but we felt that several our friends, Christian, Buddhist and Muslim, were of a mind to 'make a difference' for the common good and are in positions where they can do so. We especially noted their determination in practical ways to strengthen Ladakh's cultural and artistic heritage in the context of today's rapid development.

Delhi - Gurgaon

Delhi, or rather Gurgaon, had more good surprises in store. A small country town outside Delhi in the sixties, the massive gleaming towers of this satellite city are now home to a million and a half people. Jag Mohan Sharma was at the airport to meet us. He had been 'Best All-round Boy' in 1970 but, lacking influence, needed a word from me to get into the Engineering College. Twice he visited us in Birmingham when on attachment in the UK and in 2005 we stayed with him in Chandigarh. He was at that time responsible for the transfer of power from Kashmir into North India in summer and in the reverse direction when Kashmir freezes in winter. He had just returned from deep snow above the Banihal pass after pylons had been damaged in a freak storm. He said he could never have got up there if he had not been at our School. Now in 2012 he was General Manager of the National Power Grid and, with his wife and daughter, living in the Power Grid Township. Our stay with them included a never to be forgotten trip to Agra. I became separated from the others in the dense human tide at the unspeakably beautiful Taj Mahal. Jag Mohan called security while Catherine thought I might have fallen asleep under a tree. Meanwhile, lacking a mobile phone (every single person has one in India) I had made my way back to our taxi some distance away where the driver phoned them. The roads were crowded and bad, and the ladies were not good travellers. However, the day cemented our long friendship. Old Boys rang up and called at the flat and his wife made delicious simple meals, but mostly we just talked. Not only had our friends stayed on in Kashmir when most Hindus had left, but they both received help from and gave succour to Muslims when they in turn were in danger. The accounts of their lives were inspiring, especially Jag Mohan's perseverance and courage in supporting friends and a junior colleague, a Muslim, wrongly suspected and arrested as a militant.

Chewang's wife Yangdu lives nearby to run the business end of Rimo Travels. On our first evening she had invited us all for dinner and it was especially good to see how their daughters hit it off, both being keen students of

English literature. To share with these two families in such an elegant setting, and to think back to the past, teased the imagination.

On our last evening with Jag Mohan we went to yet another large gathering of old students, this time in an officers' mess and hosted by Major General Mohammad Amin Naik who as our schoolboy had been one of a party to climb Kolahoi back around 1970. Most of the hundred people present belonged to the *Pandit* community, exiled from Kashmir but some of them now flourishing. It was another splendid evening, though, with the men all wanting each other's news, it was rather like a noisy school class that is hard to control.

Our time was at an end, but we were to leave from another old friend's home. Living nearby was Rev Edison Noor. We had known Edison and Shymala from 1982 when they had come to Srinagar as missionaries of IEM. As a young man Edison, from the Gujarati Christian community, had been a trade unionist and something of a *goondah*. His friends were all Muslim, and when Edison turned to Christ he kept his friends and came to feel real love for Muslims. This brought him and his young family to Kashmir, but as things became difficult neighbours advised them to leave.

Edison stands in the line of those like Lesslie Newbigin in India and Kenneth Bailey in the Arab world whose lives and writing depict a Christian spirituality which draws deeply from their long immersion in non-western cultures. I can commend such a spiritual search to the loving friends, Muslim, Buddhist and Hindu, whose gracious hospitality we had so enjoyed. In the words of one of our School songs, which they raucously rendered, 'Shukar hai tera hi, Khuda.'

And so, to the Indira Gandhi International Airport, to our Emirates flight and to Birmingham. Our hearts and minds long remained in India.

5
GOLDEN DAYS IN KASHMIR

In several ways the sixties, seventies and early eighties were good times for Kashmir. Despite many problems, it was a period between the poverty of earlier days and the *zullums*, the fundamentalisms and nationalisms that have plagued us all more recently. Many, perhaps most, Kashmiris, enjoyed peace and a degree of prosperity.

Coming to Srinagar as a young and enthusiastic Principal I benefitted from both the rich tradition bequeathed by Canon Tyndale Biscoe and the educational expertise of Phil Edmonds, Principal from 1947 to 1954. Of the former, much has been written, and in 1962 was still in the hearts and minds of many who had known him. It was summed up in 1965 by Mr Sadiq, the then Chief Minister, in response to my plan to pull down the Canon's old house in the re-development of Sheikh Bagh when he referred to Biscoe as 'the founder of modern Kashmir'. But I was the immediate beneficiary of Dr Edmonds' reforms. He had disposed of all the other CMS schools, concentrating on the Hadow School as it was then known, and had retained the best of the staff, all Old Boys, and trained them to a high standard. Thus, in the core of our senior staff the School had a group of men who were both excellent teachers and deeply committed to much of the best in its tradition.

A good school can never be a one-man band, and it was teachers like Mr Salamuddin, Mr Sat Lal Razdan, Mr Amarnath, Mr Balji Saproo and Mr Kashinath Dhar who largely set the tone of the School. Along with younger masters, also Old Boys, like Mr Majid Mir, Mr Waqil and Mr David Khan, they would do anything, go anywhere, swim, climb and struggle for the School which was so central to their lives. Mr Salamuddin retired in 1971 and thereafter Mr Sat Lal was the School's lynchpin for most of the period. With his zest and enthusiasm, intellectual ability, a reflective yet practical mindset and genuine concern for all, he was outstanding. In 1964, when my contacts with the British Council were still fresh, I was able to send him for a term to Gordonstoun in Scotland. There he, as I had also earlier, benefited from Dr Kurt Hahn's inspirational legacy in a school which has amazing parallels with TBS.

So, what are our special memories, and what do they signify? Sitting with other guests at a wedding or beside another passenger in a bus I enjoyed the free-flowing conversation which so often enlightens the passing hour. The hospitality of the big formal occasions was special. One remembers traditional wedding parties: the long wait for the groom, the chanting singing of the girls, the sudden arrival of the *barat*, sometimes with the groom on his horse. There was no end to the variety of experience, days full of interests and activity in all the life of a big school where also the whole world, it sometimes seemed, would knock at the front door.

We both felt very safe. It seemed that a whole range of people, sometimes ones we hardly knew 'looked out for us', especially if there was any trouble. It could be anyone, a parent, a teacher, a neighbour, or a stranger. Doubtless sometimes it was with a measure of shared interest, as when a parent, a lady working in the telegraph office, rang me soon after 6 am to warn me that Bhutto had been executed. She knew the School might be at some risk. The day All Saints was burned in 1967, I had gone across to the house to see that the ladies were alright, I was returning when Mr Majid ran across to say, 'Don't come just yet.' I waited ten minutes before returning to find the mob had moved on, having pushed down twenty yards of the wall and smashed a lot of windows. Mr Arjan Nath the bursar was just crawling out from under his desk with a large bundle of notes he had been clutching at the moment when a brick came through the window.

As a foreigner one was conspicuous and so could attract unwelcome attention. I knew the friendliness of ordinary people in other settings where there was difficulty, such as the evening when there was a cloudburst as Catherine and I were going up to Pahalgam. Stones were falling on the road as darkness fell and I stopped the Land Rover in the village we had reached. An upstairs window opened, and we were invited in to a *Pandit* home where the large family were settling down for the night on a *wagoo* floor of the main upstairs room. Blankets were passed over and we all slept well.

It was the same on other occasions in the mountains, in situations where sharing in basic human needs for a little help or shelter somehow presents itself more naturally than in day-to-day life. Sometimes one can extend help as well as receiving it. One time in the Pir Panjal five of us returned to Yusmarg, where we had left the Land Rover, to find a desperately injured policeman. He and his bored companions had shot at a bear and wounded it, and the enraged animal had lifted his paws and ripped the flesh of his tormenter from his face down to his chest. They had no transport or telephone. We could at least hurry him to the hospital.

It is our experience of trouble, large or small, that brings us close together. The best conversation I ever had with Sheikh Sahib was such. I was to see him one day at 2 pm on some small matter. Sitting at lunch, facing out to the back garden where we had Golden Delicious apples just ready to pick, I glimpsed a boy's arm reach over the fence to detach a few. I dashed out of the front door to run around to catch him and crashed on to the stone chip path, leaving me with bleeding hands and a bruised face. Hurriedly patched up I arrived breathless and still a bit bloody. 'Mr. Ray, what *have* you done?' was the Chief Minister's incredulous greeting. He was a big man with a big laugh, and we had a good conversation about something long forgotten. He roared with laughter at my story. I guess we both had memories of years long past. Taking a few apples didn't count as stealing, in my decidedly selective boyhood judgement.

If we felt and indeed were, so accepted in Srinagar, it may have been in part that a few people at the very bottom of the social scale also knew we were there for them. One such, whom the children called the Abiguzar lady, was a poor widow with one unfortunate daughter with a disfiguring *kangri* burn. They lived in the crowded *mohalla* just across the wall, and the old lady would regularly visit Catherine for medicine or some other need.

For me some of the most special memories of those 'golden days' are times in the mountains at High Camp, at Nichinai, at Armiun or Lidderwat, perhaps best of all far up in the recesses of the Pir Panjal at Sang-i-Sufaid. Rest after long struggle, for staff as for boys, sixteen miles from Yus to High Camp at 12,000 feet, as Baba Gani or Rehman Dar coaxes tea and food from the smoky juniper-fed fire. We look out from the tent on the dazzling or tumultuous scene, sunshine or storm, beside the rushing waters of a mountain river. The last party coming up from Yus trickle in to find blankets ready for tired bodies and friends ready to receive them. A few small figures return, weary but triumphant, from some distant glacier, peak or pass.

In the mountains it is cloud and darkness, as well as the sunlit times, that have much to teach us. Modern urban life banishes both in the glare of street lighting so that the stars themselves are invisible, hardly known to today's young. One must return from the mountains to the realities of life in the city, and from journeys in the mountains to the journey of life itself. Here too cloud and darkness have much to teach us, for it is as hard and baffling experience comes along, whether sickness and bereavement or in injustice and social confusion, that we often go deeper into reality, beyond the material. But for now, I return to the happy simplicities of those days.

The sound of running water in the mountains, the whistle of the wind, the crispness of snow and the roughness of the stony track, all pass under the beauty of the sun-dappled or mist-shrouded heights above. The majesty of such a setting remains long in memory, and friendships formed there can be re-kindled long afterwards. Conversation in small groups around the fire, in the tent or on a sunny evening on the sweet grass, are relaxed and pleasant, each boy, servant or staff member having his own turn of phrase, laughter or companionable silence. Silence and sleep fall on all soon enough after a hard day. From these now distant camp scenes it is the School servants I somehow remember most clearly: Gani, Rehman Dar, Nebira and the local men: hardest worked, least paid yet irrepressible in humour and loyalty.

'Resilience and tenacity' said Khurshid Waqil, my host at the Dubai meet in 2014, when I asked him the qualities most sought for in our Old Boys. These are indeed invaluable keys to success in life. To them I would add the deep pleasure of reflection and of enduring relationship together as we explore God's beautiful world. Also, I would hope, a strong practical sense of justice, of the need to share the griefs and pains of those less fortunate, and to alleviate them where possible.

Today, worldwide, education is seen in materialistic terms, and the pressure to get that extra mark or grade drives many of the young to the limit of endurance. Yet in the real tests of life where wise judgment and decisions are needed it is character that is all important. For this no school on earth was a better nursery than TBS in those happy years.

6
PEOPLE OF KASHMIR

One might speak of 'a Kashmiri culture', but a look at the people imperfectly delineated here shows something of the variety: ethnic, religious, educational—above all personality wise—which we found in Kashmir.

Yaqub Shah

Our party of boys had walked along green lanes in the shade of scented deodars, with the rice fields of the Lolab Valley below and the forest above. We had spent the night on the floor of the old Forest Rest House at Dardapora. It was a gracious, slowly decaying building, and one imagined some long-gone Forest Officer who had delighted in this calm and beautiful place.

As we started up into the forest next morning, two bridle paths competed. To be sure of the way we asked at the last farmhouse, a long two-storey building in the Kashmiri style. At first, we could see no-one, but then a crouched figure on the balcony responded. We gathered round a man with open sores, unable to stand, covered in a torn blanket. A leper. He was unwashed and spoke with a hoarse voice. The boys gave him a good blanket, and I said that if he could get to Srinagar we would help him.

A week later, there was Yaqub Shah, sitting in his blanket on the grass in front of the house. A truck had given him a lift the sixty miles from his home. The old Mission Hospital was still open, and Donald Duck the surgeon took him for a few days to clean him up. Meanwhile we made enquiries. There is no leprosy in Kashmir, we were told. Then we learned that there was an old Leper Hospital near Nagin Lake, but no more patients were taken. Treatment was now domiciliary. We went to look. Nagin was beautiful, with the very best of the houseboats moored on its banks, the favoured resort of the most discerning visitors. The lake, fed by springs, is sparkling clean, the views are wonderful. The hum of a motor boat pulling a water skier adds a lazy drone to the scene. Visitors mainly approach by *shikara* from the Club. Certainly, no lepers in sight, and we could understand why none were wanted.

West of the lake, approached from scattered houses on the edge of the growing City, is a raised area of dry land with orchards of almond and pomegranate. Across a low fence we came to the Leper Colony. There were rows of huts, with families in and around them, and some larger buildings. All were in poor repair but occupied. Although closed to admissions, the Director of Health Services (we had been careful to include his thirteen-year-old son on our recce) agreed to an exception in Yaqub Shah's case.

With his sores treated and with clean clothing he appeared the fine man that he was. Though crippled and with limited use of his hands, there was a nobility about him. Over many years the School paid regular visits, with Yaqub as our contact. The Land Rover and trailer would be laden with boys, as we took the pipe band, and a selection of articles most wanted by the lepers. On the first such visit we were mobbed, but thereafter Yaqub established order, with children waiting in rows for shoes of the right size to be fitted. Men and women queued separately for blankets, rice, sugar, tobacco, and medicine. The latter was mainly cream for their sores. Yaqub was literate and spoke Urdu as well as Kashmiri. Many Muslims are glad to learn more about

Jesus, the healing prophet of the Quran, so long as they do not fear proselytism. I gave him a copy of St Luke's Gospel in the Urdu language.

We learned that the colony had been established by the Church Mission Society in 1891 as an arm of the Hospital at Rainawari some three miles away. The whole settlement appeared to be slowly crumbling, yet in its idyllic setting still reflected the order and care of an earlier age. There was a large hostel, now disused, for the 'clean' children of the leprosy patients, who would have been with their parents by day but slept separately to avoid contagion. There was also a long disused chapel. The settlement had reverted to the State Medical Service in the fifties. A medical orderly came at intervals with some basic drugs.

Year by year Yaqub Shah would greet us with grave courtesy and with a cheerful face, though by 1986, my last visit, his condition was very poor. He seemed accepted by the colony as its natural leader. He was—I cannot think he is still living—a person in whose frame one could only marvel at the triumph of the human spirit.

Yasin Khan

Yasin Khan is a chief among the semi nomadic *bakarwals*. His clan winter on the Indian side of the Kashmir cease-fire line in Reasi. They are a power to be reckoned with in Jammu in the winter months, with members of the State Legislative Assembly, as I was informed, among their people. In late spring they move by slow stages with their flocks and herds, their families and tents, their horses and bristling dogs, up into and through the Valley of Kashmir, and then up to their summer pastures at twelve thousand feet.

One long weekend back in the sixties a small group of our staff planned to cross from the Lidder Valley above Pahalgam to the Sind at Baltal. The weather was fine and we took no tents. We slept the first night among the pines by a *nallah* above Pahalgam and were brewing up in the morning when a heavily laden *bakarwal* caravan moved up the path beside us. Two hours later, among the topmost birches, we passed them, the men resting while the ponies grazed nearby. There were no sheep or goats, no women or children. This was the advance party going ahead to pitch camp for the ten weeks of summer. We crossed the ridge at Korapather, glimpsing the summit of Kolahoi at 18,000 feet, and had stopped for lunch on the meadow beside the stream at Vimiun, when tinkling bells again announced the *bakarwals*. Their leader asked where we were going. 'Harbhagwan.' 'Where are your tents?' 'We're sleeping rough.' 'You will sleep with us.' They went ahead at a good pace, their heavily laden mules making light of the steep climb to Har Gali. The snow lingered on the east-facing descent and as dusk fell we were glad to see their encampment among the primulas and saxifrages beyond the lake. We ate and slept well on skins in their tents. Yasin directed us on our way next morning, and it was good that he did. Broken snow bridges and dangerous ravines needed careful navigation.

Yasin Khan had enquired about the School. Sometime later a knock at our door heralded him and his brother Choudhry Iqbal. In white *shalwar*, splendid turbans and flowing beards they brought the spaces of the high pastures into our living room. Two nephews were admitted in the School. Over the years we occasionally met, usually in remote places. Many years later with our three children and two porters we had camped at 13,000 feet above the remote Wardhwan Valley. In a rainstorm at night we had been startled to hear the clatter of hooves as a party of pony men, returning to Wardhwan after the (profitable to them) Amarnath pilgrimage, nearly ran over us. 'Angrezi tambu'

(English tents), they called out of the streaming night. In the morning, just sustained by *chapatis* heated on a reluctant primus, we had clambered over Gulol Gali at 14,500 feet and were picking our way down the steep scree as a party from below came into view on their horses. Yasin Khan was at the front. 'Mr Ray!' he called out in some surprise, 'how are you here?' We conversed for a while before going our separate ways.

In 1986, hearing that we were leaving Kashmir, he called at Sheikh Bagh to say we must stay with him before we left. We agreed to go just after Eid. Catherine, our younger daughter, and I took a taxi to beyond Baltal and started to walk, rather late in the day. The way seemed steeper than twenty years earlier, and we made slow going on paths which faded into nothing as we approached the Harbhagwan gorge. Mist was gathering and the first raindrops falling when we saw a distant figure standing beside tents on the other side of the *nallah*. 'If he asks us to stay, we'll do so,' I said. As we came abreast with him the man called out, asking where we were going. 'To Yasin Khan's.' 'Dur!' (Too far!), he replied: 'Stay with me.' We were ushered into their much-patched tent and after a while offered food. It consisted of maize *chapatis* and a little sag made from dandelion and other wild plants. The two children were ragged, and the woman looked poorly. Night fell and with it came heavy rain. In our sleeping bags our daughter lay in the middle, in a growing puddle of water, while on the outside I was repeatedly trying to fend off the goats, which repeatedly succeeded in getting out of the rain.

For breakfast we were given tea and *chapati*, and as we prepared to leave had to cope with begging by our hosts. They had almost nothing, and we must have appeared very rich. We gave them some supplies and set off. The sky had cleared to a sparkling morning, and the usual profusion of mountain flowers bloomed among the rocks wherever they were out of reach of grazing. After an hour or so the path began to level off. We asked a shepherd for Yasin. 'His tents are over there, but he's away' was the reply. We found the encampment beside a stream among low ridges. A boy was herding goats and small children playing among the banks of flowers. Choudhry Iqbal greeted us with the news that Yasin had gone down to Srinagar to see us and would not be back for three days.

So, we have never, so far, seen Yasin Khan again. Iqbal gave us a tent and we stayed for two nights, welcomed, well fed and cosy in clean bedding at night. The life of the encampment, the women cooking, cleaning and tending babies, went on in traditional mode. Using juniper for fuel, Yasin Khan's wife with her beaded headgear and pewter *degchies*, was the senior figure. In the morning the teacher came for the mobile school, a group of children with their slates writing Urdu letters and figures, sitting on the turf in the shade of high mountains. We walked with Iqbal to the lake. Across the valley other herds were travelling southward. The short summer was nearing its end, and though it was still August, the following week the pastures would be empty.

Next day we walked out over the pass. Our time in Kashmir, like the *bakarwals* in the high pastures, was at an end. In a month we would be packing up and saying goodbye to friends of many years. Though we did not know it, Kashmir had troubled times ahead.

Lasa Kaul and Nagaboni

Soon after arriving in Kashmir, Catherine and I visited Lasa and his family, at Nagaboni, up a rocky track near Woyil, above the Sindh Valley along the road to Ladakh. Lasa, from a Brahmin home in Rainawari, had over the years become a dedicated and remarkable Christian during his long friendship with two independent missionary ladies, Miss Wishart and Miss Salmon.

In July of that year our first child was born with spina bifida, and Catherine went back to Scotland with her. For the next nine months I was alone in the old Principal's House at Sheikh Bagh. Lasa was my first Kashmiri friend. For much of the time he was also alone at Nagaboni, and in the hard winter of 1962-63 I stayed with him there. The snow lay deep and frozen, and the house creaked in the frosty nights. Though only about twenty-five years old, it had the feel and something of the smell of an old English farmhouse, maybe from the storeroom where apples, vegetables and dairy products were kept. It was marvellous to think that the house and the surrounding paddock, garden and orchard, even the track leading up from the Sindh Valley road, had been created from the rock-strewn hillside, the boulders gathered and piled into massive stone walls. It took little imagination to realise the labour involved by poor *gujar* and Kashmiri people, supervised by Lasa.

One January day we left the house early to climb to the ridge behind at some ten thousand feet. We saw the trail of a *gujar* dog which had been dragged off in the night by a snow leopard. Traces of blood were in the snow, and we remembered hearing barking and cries some hours earlier. We toiled up into the first scattered pine trees under a clouded winter sky, and soon entered those same clouds. The pines were white and hoar with frost. It seemed there would be no view at the summit. The cold bit our faces, but we were warm with exertion. Perhaps two hours went past, now in thicker forest, dark under the roof of fir trees. The slope finally eased, the trees thinned, and as we came towards the summit ridge a pale disc of sun appeared. Then quite quickly we were out of the cloud into brilliant sunshine. Below us lay a great heaving sea over the Sindh Valley, reaching away into the Valley of Kashmir, a mass of cloud at our feet.

Lifting our eyes, the distant ridges of the Pir Panjal, rising like the rim of a milk-filled saucer from the cloud sea, gleamed in sunlight. Nearer at hand, like islands in the sea, were the hills around Mohan Marg, beloved as a camping ground by the great anthropologist, Sir Aurel Stein. Across the valley, north-facing and dark in frozen conifers, rose the ridges leading to Mahadev mountain, now seen differently from our accustomed June approach. We rested against a tree in the warm sunlight, eating sandwiches of *lawas*, and apples from the orchard, with the sun hot enough to scent the pines, while small birds were moving around in the branches. Soon we descended into the enveloping winter cloud, back to the welcoming house, to light the oil lamps and the fire.

Over the years that followed, as our young children arrived, one of the greatest treats was always a visit in the Land Rover to Nagaboni. Our Catherine, at the age of three or four, delighted in riding Penny, the old white horse. The children enjoyed the summer fruits, and we appreciated the stillness and warmth, the views across the Valley from the window seats, and an aura of peacefulness after the busy noise of the City.

In those years Lasa was sometimes alone. Sheila and Olive, the youngest of their adopted family, were away at Avalon Training College in the Punjab, so in the holidays they would be at home. Of the two missionary ladies with whom Lasa had built Nagaboni, Miss Wishart had retired to America, but Miss Salmon was usually there.

In 1965 infiltrators from Pakistan invaded the Valley. We heard that Lasa was alone and that there had been fighting in the area. One day in August we drove out, passing numbers of troops and military vehicles, each with a machine gun mounted and ready. As we neared Nagaboni we were stopped but allowed to go on as we said we were returning at night after visiting a friend. Soldiers with headphones or larger wirelesses, and the scene in general, suggested that action was not far away.

Lasa greeted us even more warmly than usual. He was quite alone. The servant had run away a few nights earlier after hearing that a band of infiltrators, who had been eating the sheep in the government sheep farm fifteen hundred feet above the Valley, were about to attack the bridge over the Sindh. At dusk he heard them running down the track beside Nagaboni. They fired at the guards' sentry boxes on the Sindh River bridge, which they aimed to blow up. However, the soldiers had moved into trenches some distance away, and when the infiltrators advanced on to the bridge to lay a mine, they opened fire. The attackers were killed, or fled back the way they had come, up into the forest.

A year or two later, when Olive and Sheila had finished their training at Pathankot, they came to teach in our primary department. Their daily journey from Woyil, by overcrowded country bus, was slow and difficult, and after the infiltration Nagaboni was no longer so secure a home for them. It was thus a wise move, though surely undertaken with sadness, to take a rented house close to the city. It was small and cramped, and we were glad when Lasa and Miss Salmon, now with poor eyesight, built a new house in a good situation above the Dal Lake at Breinn. Then in October 1976 we said goodbye to Lasa, Miss Salmon and Olive. We have a last photograph of them with our children in the garden at Sheikh Bagh, taken as the autumn leaves fell.

When all his seven adopted children had been settled, and most of them moved to America, Lasa married Myrtle, with whom he had corresponded for twenty-five years.

They settled in Myrtle's childhood home, Spokane in America's Pacific north-west. Lasa wrote that Spokane was like Kashmir, with its apple orchards. It was there that we went to visit them another quarter century later, and to stay with Olive and her American husband near Seattle.

We returned from America on 10 September 2001, arriving in Birmingham next morning, 'Nine Eleven'.

Sofi

Mr GM Sofi was the owner and editor of the *Srinagar Times*. His office was right beside us, opposite the Girls' School, down the lane from Lal Chowk, and we would hear him arriving on his motor scooter. Everyone who wanted to keep up with affairs read his paper, and many feared his exposés. His brother, the photographer and cartoonist for the paper, pictured a leading politician slapping a policeman across his face. The politician resigned next day.

We all knew Sofi as a ubiquitous figure who, welcome or unwelcome, might appear on any occasion from a wedding to a trial. No-one refused admission to Mr Sofi. I first met him face to face during the School strike in 1973. School was closed, the striking staff had unflattering banners along the roadside and I was alone in the house. The bell rang and there was Sofi. I said, 'We don't want publicity.' He laughed. 'Have a look on the roadside: "British Dogs Go Home!" You've got publicity anyway. I'll tell your side of the story.' So, he came in. We drank coffee and he told my side of the story very faithfully.

Our next encounter was different. I had flown back from Amritsar to find Miss Gergan, Headmistress, waiting to see me. She had a copy of the *Srinagar Times* announcing the new 'Biscoe and Mallinson Schools Parents Association', formed to remedy a list of misdoings which, she informed me, had grown each of the days I had been away.

Sofi had begun to bring his daughter to the School on his scooter, arriving just when it suited him to get to his office. This was usually rather later than the morning class roll call. He had, it seemed, had this routine for some time. After all, no-one challenged Sofi. But Miss Gergan was another matter. The child must be punctual or leave. So, the first headline had claimed that, 'in spite of the extortionate fees charged by the School, no seat was provided' for his daughter. Next day the news was of a racket being operated by the School, overcharging as well as failing to provide furniture. Then the latest was that the School was giving Christian teaching to Muslim girls.

Serious stuff! Sofi and a representative of the Biscoe and Mallinson Schools Parents' Association were coming to see us at lunchtime. They arrived, looking very pleased until we said that we didn't recognise their Association. Next morning the *Times* announced an open meeting of the Parents' Association in Pratap Park on Saturday to protest against the lengthening catalogue of our evil deeds. The park was just opposite the Boys' School, beside the bus station where a crowd of loiterers so easily becomes a mob. The incendiary possibilities were obvious.

I have no sense of triumph in what followed. If anyone it was Miss Gergan who won the day, but perhaps the credit is not to any of us. We prayed, and it rained so much that by Friday there were two inches of water in Pratap Park. So, along with further allegations, the protest meeting was postponed till the following Saturday. Still it rained, and still fresh allegations were produced. By the next Thursday, with water still standing, the *Srinagar Times* announced that the meeting would now be held in the lounge of the Crown Hotel. No incendiary possibilities there.

On Friday two Old Boys, good cricketers and young parents, came to see me saying they would go along to the meeting and let me know what happened. It seemed that the public had begun to feel the catalogue of our misdoings was just a bit overdone. The lads returned smiling to say that total numbers had been thirteen. Without Sofi and his brother, and the two of them, aggrieved parents had thus been in single figures, out of a possible total of over four thousand.

Many years later, on our return visit to Kashmir in 2005, someone met me in the street and said, 'You were the only one who ever got the better of Sofi!' That's not how I felt about it. But we had prayed. I liked Sofi, a genuine bright Kashmiri if ever there was one.

Alas, Sofi is no longer among us and Srinagar is the poorer for his passing, I see no reference in recent days to his paper, which was so eagerly passed from one person to another. He was assuredly one of the City's characters for many years.

Abdul Gani Ladakhi: School servant, neighbour and friend

Gani, broad shouldered and imperturbable, stood across the small swing gate as the mob came down Residency Road, having burned All Saints Church for the second time. The leaders paused for a moment. 'What do you people want?' asked Gani, not moving.

'Jalaou, Jalaou! (Burn it!) answered the crowd. 'Burn it if you like,' replied Gani, still not moving, 'but it's your School.' The mob hesitated, then moved off to burn something else.

Though most of the boys came daily from all parts of Srinagar, there was a hostel for those from Ladakh and other faraway places. Abdul Gani was for many years the Hostel Cook. One entered the hostel through the kitchen, so was greeted by him. Wielding his ladle with quiet authority Gani was simply one of the most reliable and competent men I have known, trusted by the boys, by their parents and by all who knew him. Over the two weeks of

School Camp in July, he would oversee the kitchen, and an enduring memory is of him at High Camp, under a tarpaulin at twelve thousand feet in some remote valley. Whether conjuring fire from smoky juniper, supervising his assistants as they dismembered a goat or serving curry in a rainstorm to eighty hungry boys, no task seemed beyond this vital member of the School community.

When the High Commission in Delhi asked me to extract a young British woman 'believed forcibly held on houseboat Queen of the Valley' he was the obvious man to take along. No one was going to tangle with him.

Gani was of a Ladakhi Muslim family and lived in a small quarter behind Miss Mallinson's house. Mrs Gani was from Kishtwar, a mountainous region in the Pir Panjal. Their six children grew up with our three. Being at the heart of our small resident community along with the hostel boys—the School was empty of day children and staff by 5 pm and at weekends—it was the Ladakhis whom we got to know best, along with a few children of resident staff. The smaller ones played their make-believe games in the back garden. Football, swimming and just hanging out together, enduring friendships grew up and outlasted our return to Britain in 1986.

Relationships started early. On one occasion Gani's second daughter came to the door. 'Come quickly, Mummy's baby's coming!' Not having expected to attend the delivery, Catherine hurried over with thread and scissors hastily sterilised in the pressure cooker to find that the baby, a boy, had already arrived. Thirty years later during our 2012 visit, now one of our teachers, he said to her, 'You should remember me; you delivered me!' The Ganis were educated by the School and have flourished. Mrs Gani mothered not only her own large family, but the small Ladakhi boys as well.

Gani himself moved into the School as office peon or orderly. In a big school this included being a kind of gatekeeper, sifting requests or demands for access. Apart from the time when he turned the mob away there were other occasions when rioting students poured down the road to be met by police or paramilitary in Lal Chowk. Gani always gave us sufficient warning. His growing family finally found better accommodation, a quarter in the old Turkestani Sarai, the terminus for more than a century of the caravan route from Central Asia.

Gani and Mrs Gani have passed on, and their eldest son Ghulam had died in a truck accident on the Zoji La some years earlier. In 2011 our daughter visited Ladakh and happily followed up those childhood memories of games in the back garden. A year later Catherine and I visited Suraya and Anita in their homes in the old alleyways of Leh, and met Jamila and Munir, both now teachers, in Srinagar. Jamila, with her own family and still living in the City, was rescued by the army from her home in the terrible floods of September 2014 and is a teacher in the Biscoe School.

Doctor Naseer Ahmed Shah, Dr Girija Dhar and Miss Mahmooda Ahmed Ali Shah

After twenty-four years in Kashmir, and for reasons which there is no need to detail here, I was handed a short note from the State Home Department. It read, 'You are hereby required to quit India forthwith.' A strengthening word came from a friend: 'See Isaiah chapter 52, verse twelve.' Then I went to meet Dr Naseer and showed him the order. He laughed and said, 'You won't leave India so easily as that. Who have you got in the School?' I mentioned the sons of the State Congress chief, and of a Central Government minister. Naming them he said the one would not be useful, but the other could help. Then he wrote and addressed a note. 'And take this,' he said, 'to the Private Secretary to the Prime Minister.' To do so took some perseverance. It was not easy for a foreigner to gain admission, even with such a note in my hand, to Rajiv Gandhi's office in New Delhi. 'I think it will be all right, Mr Ray' was the young secretary's smiling response after reading the letter.

Dr Naseer had long been a true friend. Some years earlier he had been sitting beside me at a public function when a local politician, an Old Boy and also a near neighbour who perhaps had his eye on some of our extremely valuable land, proposed setting up an Old Boys' Association. 'Be very careful,' whispered Naseer.

'Don't offer to do anything, let him take the initiative. It will come to nothing.'

There were other small crises when Dr Naseer was our immediate recourse. We occasionally bought honey from a villager who would come with combs dripping from a wicker basket carried on his head. On this occasion the honey, mingled with pollen, set up an acute allergy when I incautiously swallowed a mouthful. The inside of my mouth and throat swelled until I could scarcely breathe. I was on the verge of choking, and it was only later that my wife said she was ready to do a tracheotomy with a kitchen knife, should that be an urgent lifesaving necessity. An antihistamine tablet and a speedy drive took us to Dr Naseer, whose remedy was fortunately sufficient. We had found him in his small consulting room, crowded with poor folk, at Dal Gate. His skills were known to all. Charging the rich, he gladly served the poor for little or nothing.

Naseer was one of a remarkable family who set the highest standards for public service in this State most mired in corruption. His sister Mahmooda became the very distinguished Principal of the recently formed Government College for Women, and a wonderful friend and ally. She lived at great personal cost, never married and endured ridicule and worse for her dignified stand for the true equality of her sex. She was a founder member in 1962 of our joint Governing Body and could be severe. As a newcomer I was in awe of this delightful but regal lady who had the ear of Indira Gandhi. In the City the CMS Girls' School was always called 'the Mission School'. To my western consciousness this suggested a bygone colonialism, but to my proposal that a new name should move away from such foreign dependency Mahmooda replied with scorn, 'Only one name is possible for this School.'

A strong Congress supporter, she faced danger as well as difficulty in the years after we left in 1986. In 2005 we visited her both in Jammu and then in her Gagribal home in Srinagar. Even then an armed guard was on duty at the gate as was still the case seven years later when we last met.

Naseer himself is an FRCP of both Edinburgh and London. While in London he had met and married Dr Girija Dhar. Girija was from a leading Kashmiri *Pandit* family, and related to DP Dhar, the then Indian Ambassador in Moscow. A marriage involving prominent Brahmin and Muslim families could have caused a storm in Srinagar, but as it was far away, disapproval was muted. Applause would have been more appropriate, as few more valuable citizens could be imagined. For some years one was Principal of the Medical College while the other was Superintendent of the Women's Hospital. Girija vowed to bring the standards of Barts Hospital to Srinagar. She lost a few battles but kept her vision. Patients relied on their relatives bringing food for them, even cooking with primus stoves in the wards. All attempts to introduce food supplied from the hospital kitchens failed, as families only trusted their own members. Trust was indeed in short supply, as seen when some nurses sold injections, injecting patients with water. The hospital reverted to a system where families bought their medicines from the chemist's shop, watching closely during administration.

Dr Naseer built a pleasant house above the Dal Lake. It was there we spent our last evening before finally leaving Kashmir in 1986. In return for my services as Unofficial Representative (Honorary Consul) the High Commission in Delhi had from time to time sent an occasional carefully wrapped package of single malt, which remained untouched save for special occasions. This was clearly one such, and it was good to leave the remaining packages with a discerning recipient.

In 2005 we met again, not in Kashmir but in Liverpool, where Naseer and Girija were visiting their daughter and son-in-law, doctors in the University Hospital. At home in Kashmir, guards had long been posted at their gate: Girija had narrowly escaped when militants opened fire and shattered the car's windscreen as she was driving through her hospital gate.

It was our great privilege to dine in their pleasant home once again in 2012 in a Kashmir still watchful, but more relaxed. That visit was to mark the Centenary of the CMS School for Girls, since 1962 renamed the Mallinson Girls' School at Mahmooda's insistence. On that occasion Catherine was a guest of honour, Dr Farooq Abdullah, now a minister in the Union Government, presided, and Mahmooda, sadly frail in old age, was justly honoured as the one who had for a further half century taken forward Miss Mallinson's work of uplift for Kashmiri Muslim women.

7
SIX CHIEF MINISTERS

'**K**ashmir is run by the BBC,' I was told on our arrival in Srinagar in January 1962. Even given the reputation for objectivity the BBC then enjoyed that was surprising news until I understood that BBC stood for the Bakshi Brothers Corporation, Bakshi being the Prime Minister.

During our quarter century in Kashmir in one sense I was powerless. We could have been sent packing at any time on the word of anyone who exploited our previous service in Pakistan, or of a bishop who felt it was high time an Indian national was running the School. The British Empire had long gone, and there was no gunboat down the river. Yet we and our children lived in the centre of that Central Asian city feeling entirely secure and with cordial relationships with all manner of neighbours from the very rich to the poorest. We educated the children of many of our neighbours and our rulers and so, if not power, had influence. What I said in Assembly or wrote in the *Biscoe Bugle* went back via the children to their parents. More important was the way the School functioned. In a society where much was hidden, we were an open book. Thus, we were in a situation of privilege and even sometimes intimacy with leaders in society as well as a great number of citizens of all classes, faiths and attitudes.

During those years, of the seven Chief Ministers of the Indian state of Jammu and Kashmir six had their children in the School, or were Old Boys, or both. The wives of several were Old Girls. When in 1965 I wanted to pull down Canon Biscoe's decaying old house to use the space for school development, the then CM, Mr Sadiq, said in front of two or three thousand Kashmiris that in his view 'the house of the founder of modern Kashmir should be an *astaan*, a shrine.' The heads of nine government departments, I was told soon after my arrival as Principal, were Old Boys.

In 1962 Ghulam Mohammed Bakshi was Prime Minister. A lot of money did run out at the corners, but Bakshi himself, confident and thrusting, was able to take forward some of Sheikh Abdullah's good development projects. Unfortunately, though perhaps inevitably, he established what became almost the foundation of Kashmir policy, securing assistance from Delhi on the basis of an assertion of loyalty which went beyond the feelings of Kashmiri people. Loyalty cannot be bought, and the sense of this demeaning bargain was a factor in the breakdown of 1989, after we had left. This is especially sad as Kashmiris, following Sheikh Abdullah in the decades after 1947, well understood that their larger interest, if not their hearts, lay with a 'secular, democratic and socialist' India. Before entering politics Bakshi had briefly taught in the School and was well known to our staff. He had also, though it was not widely known, been baptised by Jock Purvis of the Central Asia Mission, some time before 1947. Canon Biscoe had said he could teach in the School, whether as a Muslim or a Christian, but he had to make up his mind which.

My first meeting with this powerful man, as a young and inexperienced foreign Head of the School, was tricky. On arrival I had found myself responsible, not just for the Boys' School but also for the Girls'. In the same year the much-loved Muriel Mallinson, who had been the main source of uplift for Kashmiri Muslim women for nearly forty years, retired. She had just brought her school, or at least its teachers, from the old City to a large vacant house in Sheikh Bagh beside the growing Boys' School. Her teachers were mature ladies and were all her Old Girls. They were matriculates at most, having grown up when there had been virtually no education for Muslim women. But by 1962 there was an excellent Government College for women, producing graduate teachers. Thus, very few children made the journey up from Fateh Kadal, but the teachers all came, wanting their salaries. Often there were few girls to teach, but to sit in the shade of the *chenar* trees was a pleasant change from Fateh Kadal. The face of Miss Mallinson's faithful Munshi Nand Lal grew more and more despondent as the bank balance shrank towards zero. Action was inevitable, so reluctantly I terminated the services of the seven most senior. They went with loud cries to Mrs Sadiq, fellow Old Girl and wife of the Minister for Education. When he declined to see them, they went on to their classmate, Mrs Bakshi. She sent them to her husband, who summoned me. We had a short conversation. Bakshi Sahib, as we called him, said, 'Mr Ray, the seven sisters you sent away are very unhappy. I advise you to take them back.' I replied in a rather Kashmiri manner, 'I will do as you advise, Sir, but we have no money.' He said he would give us ten thousand rupees to get started, and all was well. He came as Chief Guest on Parents' Day and advised us publicly to 'build or bust'.

I next met him during our annual camp in the mountains when a disastrous flood hit the area. A hotel in the nearby resort of Pahalgam was swept into the river and a number of people had died. Our boys were all safe in their tents when Bakshi turned up and told us to pack up and send the children back. I protested, but he said, 'There's panic in Srinagar; they won't believe their children are safe unless they see them.' I then went with him as he supervised labourers clearing the road in a half-hearted way. He stopped the car, picked up a mattock and started swinging it with vigour. 'Like this!' he said. I thought to myself, what Chief Minister except an Old Boy of ours would swing a pick like that? Bakshi was generally liked, but his cousin Rashid, it seemed, was less popular.

Rashid Bakshi was at that time the Indian representative to the United Nations. India, with Egypt and Yugoslavia, was a leading non-aligned state. It suited New Delhi to have a Kashmiri and a Muslim in such a symbolic post. Responding to a friendly greeting as he was collecting his son one day, I invited him round for a cup of tea. Next day Pir Salamuddin, Vice Principal, Old Boy—and *Pir*—said, unusually sharply, 'You should *never* invite a man like that into your home!' Thus, I began to learn caution.

By the time we returned from leave in March 1965 Mr GM Sadiq had taken Bakshi's place as Chief Minister. Mr Sadiq, whom I instinctively liked, was an Old Boy with two good sons in the School. He was called a communist, but it seemed to me that his socialism and strong sense of justice owed more to Canon Biscoe than to his stay in Moscow. The change in government was quickly seen in increased emphasis on health and education. He set a personal example in his modest spending on a family wedding and would often refer in public to Canon Biscoe and the social transformation wrought by the School. When the old Rainawari Mission Hospital had to be handed to government as the Indian Church could not find suitable staff to replace overseas mission personnel he insisted on one condition in granting compensation. This was that the money be spent on the continuing Christian hospital at Anantnag, which was gladly done. At a tea party to mark the handover Mr Sadiq expressed the hope that under government control the same spirit of service would continue as in the past when every operation was preceded by prayer.

I remember, in a Moral Science class, saying that Sadiq Sahib was giving Kashmir a health and education service, but the rats were eating the flesh off the bones. But when I became too moralistic a boy, the son of a politician, said, 'Sir, if our fathers didn't make a little extra money, we couldn't come to this School!' So perhaps we were all complicit.

I had had reason to call on Sadiq very soon after returning from leave in March 1965. It was our last voyage by ship, and part way down the Red Sea the steward handed me a telegram at dinner 'SCHOOL BURNED DOWN RETURN IMMEDIATELY.' The captain helped me get a flight from Aden to Bombay, so I was quickly back to find classes carrying on in every odd corner: doubling up in Junior School rooms, the garage and the Hostel. Catherine had stayed on the ship and went ashore when it called at Karachi to meet Scottish friends. There she learned of Pakistani newspaper reports that the School had been burned in the course of riots. But there had been no riots, and the fire had started under the wooden staircase at night. The Presentation Convent also had a mysterious fire a week later, so we tended to wonder whether Pakistani agents, preparing for the Infiltration which led to war the following August, were trying to spread a picture of non-existent trouble, especially in places where publicity would be gained by the presence of foreign nationals. In any event, Mr Sadiq was very supportive, as were Old Boys, of our rebuilding.

Sadiq had cause to summon Heads of Schools and Colleges together in another fire-related matter a little later. Kashmir was, and still will be, a fertile field for rumour, *hoosh moosh*, sometimes manipulated to cause maximum panic. On this occasion, apparently following the elopement of a Brahmin girl with a Muslim boy (or was there some other cause?; in Kashmir it is hard to discern the truth of a matter) a rash of fires sprang up.

So Sadiq called a meeting to remind heads of their duty to ignore rumour. 'If you hear that a mosque has been burned at Anantnag or a temple set on fire at Sopore, get on with your work. It is for the Police to deal with any miscreants.' Then, typically, he added, 'When I was in School it was rumoured that there were *djinns* in the River and all traffic (the Jhelum River carried the City's commerce) stopped. The City was at a standstill. Mr Biscoe ordered ten of us—I was one of them—to jump off Amirakadal bridge into the river and swim under the seven bridges to Chattabal. All eyes were upon us from every bridge and window to see if the *djinns* would get us. When we climbed out at Chattabal trade resumed as normal.'

One often felt the privilege of trust from men like Sadiq, who sadly died in office, to be succeeded by Sayed Mir Qasim. Javed, Mir Qasim's son, was an intelligent lad from a traditional family. He swam the Dal Lake, climbed Mahadev and was a model pupil. The first time I asked to see his father was on being handed a copy of *Blitz*, the Bombay scandal sheet. Under the heading 'Missionary Spies Active in Kashmir' I was cast as leader of a group connected with everything from the CIA to forcible conversions and the Prophet's Hair Agitation. Concerned, I took the paper to Mir Qasim who smiled as he read it. He said, 'I've been in *Blitz* two or three times. It's quite an honour. Is your conscience clear? Then you have nothing to fear.' We chatted briefly, and he said in parting, 'If I was you I would look in your staffroom.'

He was, of course, right. Most of our senior staff were Old Boys with great loyalty to the School and a willingness—even a delight—in taking part in our swims, mountain camps and climbs. They also exhibited something of Canon Biscoe's Christian ethic of service in the community, all combined with their conservative Brahmin homes: a surprising mix! The younger staff, however, were not Old Boys. Most of them also gave of their best, but naturally they looked to their future and some, perhaps, hoped the School, like a golden apple, would fall into their hands when the last overseas Principal (myself) left. The old CMS Central High School at Fateh Kadal had been given to its teachers, so why not TBS?

Our Chairman, the Bishop of Amritsar of the Church of North India, had other ideas, and began to seek a fit national Christian, if possible a Kashmiri, to continue the work begun in a different era. Not surprisingly the conflict of interest led to the one strike I have ever known, skilfully exploited by two or three persons, who joined hands with the All J& K Low-Paid Workers Association to produce an interesting situation. Management closed the School early for the summer break: the strikers, in defiance, said the School would stay open, and we had what in Kashmir would be called a *tamasha*. So, I went to see Mr Mir Qasim again. He simply asked what he could do to help. I passed on local management's request that the State Government appoint a Commission of Enquiry.

In the event it all turned out for the best, and remarkably even relationships within the School suffered no long-term harm. It transpired that parents, Old Boys and government all wanted us to run the School, rather than a group of our teachers. But, as in so many situations one had to stand and put it to the test.

More influential with Kashmiris than any of the Ministers I had known, whether in power or in prison, was Sheikh Abdullah, the Lion of Kashmir. It was he who from 1931 had fought for the cause of Kashmiri Muslim people, and he had found an ally in Canon Biscoe. Coming to power as Prime Minister at Partition he had resisted the claims of Pakistan, and when the Hindu Maharajah had fled, had rallied the State militia against the Pathan raiders. He was realist enough to know that a separate independent Kashmir, which might be his desire, would soon be swallowed up by any of its three powerful neighbours.

His two sons were boys in the School under Dr Phil Edmonds, a dynamic Australian CMS missionary. Sheikh Sahib appreciated his educational gifts and involved him in the foundation and development of Kashmir University. Dr Edmonds thus inevitably became too close to political leadership, so when Sheikh Abdullah was ousted by the more right-wing Congress leaders in 1953, and put in prison in South India, Dr Edmonds was also out of favour. He went to Pakistan and ran Edwardes College in Peshawar so well that Bhutto was unable to nationalise it twenty years later. Edmonds was also an admirer of Kurt Hahn and Gordonstoun and it was he who suggested in 1959 that TBS might be the place where God might be calling us to serve.

When we arrived in 1962 Sheikh Sahib was still in custody, and the first member of the family we met was his son Farooq, who had qualified as a doctor in England. Somewhere around 1970 he came to introduce us to his wife, Molly, who wanted some reassurance that Kashmir was a good place to live. We said we had found it so! Sometime later Sheikh was permitted to return to Kashmir. Large numbers gathered on the School frontage as his motorcade was expected. Usually we kept clear of crowds, but this was clearly a relaxed occasion, so Catherine and our three small children joined me at the roadside fence. As Sheikh came alongside, Farooq saw us, stopped the car and got out to greet us very warmly. It was clear that the Abdullah family saw us as friends and allies. Bearing in mind Phil Edmonds' history we kept a distance from all political figures, but it is always good to know that authority is appreciative.

In due course Mr Mir Qasim stepped aside and Sheikh returned to general, though not universal, rejoicing. As the one who had struggled with the Dogra Maharaja for the Kashmiris from 1931 he had immense personal authority and had after Partition led them into unheard of prosperity.

A chief instigator of the 1973 School strike, a teacher, had disappeared the day after Mrs Gandhi declared her 'Emergency' in 1975 and was finally dismissed as being absent without leave. He was apparently wanted by the police as a member of a proscribed right-wing group. After the Emergency was ended I was asked to take him back by the State Education Department. Then came a more ominous enquiry from the Union Home Ministry. I was concerned when one evening the phone rang. 'Sheikh here, Mr Ray, you have dismissed Mr X. Can you tell me why?' I told him. He thanked me, and I heard no more.

In Kashmir a breakdown of law and order, however manipulated, is the occasion for settling grudges. That April we heard that former President Bhutto was to be executed in Rawalpindi. Bhutto had never while alive seemed of interest to Kashmiris, but news of his death was the signal for a vast mob to assemble on the Polo Ground. Whatever the instigators' intent, three days of mayhem followed. On the first day a section of the crowd burned All Saints Church, rebuilt after the 1967 fire, and attacked the Catholic Church and the United Nations office. Curfew was declared. On the third day large numbers of villagers had their homes burned.

We came to know of this when the National Christian Council of India, sent to enquire about the church, offered money for rebuilding. Pastor Yonathan said he would not accept any unless the more numerous Muslim village sufferers were also helped. A good amount was sent and with it the School was asked to buy cooking pots, rice and other necessities for the homeless families. In School I asked each boy to contribute through the Poor Fund, or give a blanket. Parents, usually generous, gave nothing. The cause was unpopular! Two busloads of children went with the supplies we had bought, which we took to a village forty miles distant. Senior staff worked with the *Tehsildar* to distribute necessities to the affected families while I walked up the street to find a group of chilly young men beside some tents. 'Where has all this come from?' one of them asked. 'I'm from England,' I said, 'but these supplies have come from Christians in India.' After a pause I added, 'Our churches got burned down too. We're a minority and sometimes these things happen. But you are all Muslims so why did you suffer?' His reply was highly enlightening, but I will not print it here.

A very different occasion was when the phone rang from Sheikh Sahib's home. Begum Abdullah asked for Mrs Ray with the request, to our great surprise, that she receive Edward Heath, who until recently had been the UK Prime Minister, at the airport. Farooq had met him somewhere in the Commonwealth and invited him to visit Kashmir, but he was arriving at an awkward time between ministries, and we were seen as safe neutral figures to host him.

In 1980 the School welcomed people from across the world to its Centenary. For its planning committee I sat opposite Bashir Bakshi, Javed Mir Qasim, Rafiq Sadiq and Farooq Abdullah, sons of four Chief Ministers. One of them looked around and said, 'So long as we stick together, nothing much can go wrong in Kashmir!' They were, alas, mistaken. The Centenary Celebrations under the beautiful *chenar* trees of Sheikh Bagh were a great success, with Old Boys coming from across the world, yet within ten years the Kashmiri Brahmin minority, who had for centuries clung to their homes so tenaciously, would be virtually gone from their ancestral land, and the whole of society would be plunged into such miseries as were to follow.

Many years later, on a second return visit after our departure in 1986, we met Umar Abdullah, Farooq's son. The atmosphere was relaxed but his chief concern was the endemic corruption. He spoke of the huge amounts misappropriated in the course of construction of the new trunk road from Qazigund to Baramulla. To my enquiry as to whether the rogues could not be caught he replied that it was easy to get them but recovering the money was a different matter. 'Plus ça change, plus c'est la même chose,' I thought. We sensed an able and effective lead from the third generation of a remarkable family. The catastrophic floods of September 2014, with seventeen feet of water in the School grounds, for the time being swept his administration away, but given the ebb and flow of politics, he will probably be back in due course.

No Chief Minister alone can rid Kashmir of the corruption which is so often a prime cause of breakdown and revolution, though it may come under a political or religious cover. A culture of civic honesty, replacing that of financial corruption, may be an essential in recovering hope for Kashmir. The name of Chimed Gergan on the School Honours board is a lonely one, and it is worth telling his story. He is cited as 'having given his life for the purity of the public service in Kashmir'. Chimed, as a Forest Officer in Zanskar, apprehended a gang of *khat* smugglers and took them to Kargil to face justice. The judge was corrupt and let them off, so the next year they were unafraid when he again tried to catch them, and they murdered him. Biscoe, seeking some retribution, obtained his post for his younger brother, the late Mr SS Gergan, who we later knew as game warden in the Forestry Department. Will some of the old students of our Schools, not only Biscoe-Mallinson, but others of similar heritage, be able to share in an effective lead to clean up the system today? We can all in a small way help towards this so that all Kashmiris will share in the peace and security that India at its best can provide.

Mention of Chimed Gergan in the last chapter, and aware of the great damage done to the people of Kashmir by the greed which is the cause of corruption, makes this the natural point to place Dr Jyoti Sahi's little drawings of the Kashmir scene. These he made for the School nearly fifty years ago to illustrate the story of Zacchaeus.

In this story Jesus calls Zacchaeus, a wealthy chief tax collector who wanted to see Jesus as he passed by with his followers. But Zacchaeus, being a small man, had to climb a tree to see him. Jesus looked up and told him to come down as, he said, 'I must stay at your house today.' Zacchaeus gladly welcomed him in, but the crowd complained that Jesus was welcoming a sinner (tax collectors were often corrupt and anyway collected for the hated Romans). Zacchaeus, however, said to Jesus, 'Here and now I give half my possessions to the poor, and if I have cheated anybody I will give back four times the amount.' Jesus replied, 'Today salvation has come to this house because this man, too, is a son of Abraham. For the son of man came to seek and to save what was lost.' See pp I to X after folio number 76.

8
The Mallinson Girls' School and Miss Gergan

My memories of the Girls' School will always be interlinked with Miss Premi Gergan. One could almost say that she re-founded the School, because in 1962 when I took over the Boys' School from Eric Tyndale Biscoe, Miss Mallinson was on the point of retiring after over forty years of the most wonderful service, and the School, using a few rooms in Barton House, seemed like an orphan. There were all Miss Mallinson's old teachers, loyal to her memory and bereft of her presence. None were graduates. A small number of girls had followed the teachers up from Fateh Kadal a few months earlier. There was no money and, if memory is correct, no uniform. I found myself Principal with no means of doing an effective job and just coming to grips with the Boys' School.

What enabled us to survive was the huge reputation and the strong desire of so many, from the Chief Minister to the Principal of the Government College for Women, Miss Mahmooda Ahmed Ali Shah, to see her School flourish. Before she left Muriel Mallinson said to me, 'I did not come to Srinagar to run a school, but to be with the women of this city when they needed help.' People still living will speak of her with the utmost affection. With her fluent Kashmiri she was simply loved by the people she gave her life to serve.

Thus, we staggered on, much helped by Miss Demta from Bihar, until word came that Miss Premi Gergan, MA, Dip. Ed, who was lecturing in a leading women's college in Calcutta, was ready to give up that post to join us in Srinagar. From then until after our Centenary in 1980, she was my principal colleague as she steadily transformed the School. I remained Manager, but with poise and dignity she was totally in charge as we sought together to build a new school. Much helped by old students of both schools as well as by government, a good classroom block was erected in 1965. A Lower Primary Department was built, many of the materials coming from Canon Biscoe's old house, and a Girls' School field was made from the paddocks and gardens which had belonged to Biscoe's and Barton's houses. A Hall with classrooms below followed in 1974. The beautiful *chenar* trees made a fine backdrop for the growing school.

From the moment she joined us the attitude expressed by Premi was of a school which aims for the highest. Morning Assembly set the tone for the day: serious, dignified and purposeful. The Boys' School seemed rather 'rough and ready' by comparison, somewhat lacking in refinement and the higher aspects of culture. By contrast, of the Girls' one remembers the long succession of Variety Concerts in the Tagore Hall, with what was to me an astonishingly beautiful and polished display of Indian classical dancing. In Art also there was something of a cultural tradition. This was centred in Hajra Begum and enriched by Miss Palin, a friend of Miss Mallinson whose paintings of beautiful Kashmir mountain flowers are in the Victoria and Albert Museum in London.

There were also activities shared with the boys, such as the annual dramas, often a shortened Shakespeare, performed in the Girls' School Hall. Not to be outdone, the girls also camped and climbed with vigour. When Major (later General) Nugyal and Captain (later Brigadier) Prem

The followers of Jesus were tall

But Jesus loves small people

Zacchaeus was so small

How could Zacchaeus see over the tall, proud, crowding people?

IV

Like a child he ran ahead and climbed a tree

V

Jesus asked Zacchaeus to come down as he wanted to come to his house

VI

And though everyone said he was a sinner
because he cheated people, Jesus went to his house

Zacchaeus had a big house and a guilty heart,
but it changed when Jesus came

*He decided to give lots of money to the poor and
pay back what he had stolen*

And he showed he had a big enough heart to be truly humble!

Chand led our party of seven to the summit of Kolahoi there were five boys and two girls.

It was so fitting that brothers and sisters could come to school together. The distinctive uniform was introduced and has remained the same. It was a great pleasure after school to walk across the Girls' field to the Principal's house as the girls passed by, often collecting a small brother on the way. Sometimes, if there had been a cookery lesson, one was surrounded by a gang of juniors, and not released until one had sampled a large number of pakoras or other delicacies

Apart from Miss Gergan's personal qualities, she came from a family that had been linked with the School almost throughout its existence. Joseph Gergan, her grandfather who translated the Bible into Tibetan, was among the first boys in the School hostel. The story of her uncle Chimed is commemorated on the honours board as having given his life for the purity of the public service. Her maternal grandmother had been an early Inspectress of Girls' Schools in Kashmir. The links continue, for Premi's younger brother, the Rev Elijah Gergan, who was in our year ten in 1963, has only just (2017) given up his role as Principal of the Moravian School in Leh.

In 1980 Miss Gergan wished to resign to follow a strong sense that she should work for the Pentecostal Church to which she owed her loyalty. In retrospect I should not have stood in her way by persuading her to stay as we had serious difficulties later. But Miss Premi Gergan was such a figure that all who knew her will remember her with the greatest respect, and I am so grateful to God that we parted on good terms. She sadly died at a fairly young age in 2003. My memories of her will always be of her leading her school with great distinction, courage and success.

When we revisited Kashmir for the Girls School Centenary in 2012, Mrs Ray was a Guest of Honour.

Mahmooda in her old age was honoured for her large part in carrying forward the work of women's advancement that Miss Mallinson had started. At a crowded, noisy and joyful occasion in the newly refurbished Indoor Stadium we were treated to an excellent cultural show—by the boys and girls jointly. It was Mrs Joyce Kaul and forty school servants who had cleared the stadium of rubbish after years of occupation by the security forces.

At the 2012 Centenary event in the School I was very impressed by the keenness of senior girls' involvement with the IYA, the Indian branch of the International Youth Award for Young People, with its threefold stress on community service, acquiring useful skills and an adventurous expedition. I was especially pleased as this all springs from Gordonstoun, and from its founder Dr Kurt Hahn. He had, as mentioned earlier, been my role model in education since first appointing me in 1953 as the initial Expeditions Master at Gordonstoun: the very beginning of Adventure Education.

At the same celebration we were given a deeply thoughtful address by Wajahat Habibullah, the then Chairman of the National Commission for Minorities. A former IAS officer of long experience which was mainly in Kashmir, he has always held that Kashmir's belonging can only be with India. His recent writings, however, such as *My Kashmir*, seem to lack hope politically, though in fact his book makes it clear that there are potential grounds for renewed hope.

In this age women's education and the struggle for recognition of full and equal humanity has led to great benefits for all. The mainly male leaders of the nations having so failed in making and keeping the peace, can women share more fully in helping us recover our humanity across the divisions of race, religion and history?

This may or may not be primarily political. If women are especially the guardians of the young, those to whom we specially look for care and kindness, they can also come to the fore as protectors of our environment. In 2012, flying into the Valley, it seemed that uncontrolled greed and development, joining village to village and house to house, was ruining the beauty of Kashmir. 'If there is heaven on earth, it is this, it is this' reads like a mockery amid the fumes of diesel and smog which obscure the mountains, and the cacophony of noise which banishes peace. With ribbon development from Tangmarg to Ganderbal, it is late in the day to institute measures to protect natural beauty and life itself. Gone are the days when a little corruption in the Forest Department, the cutting of trees illegally, could be overlooked. The 2014 floods were a warning. They should not be a foretaste of worse to come. We knew enough professional people of real public spirit, many of them our Old Boys and Old Girls, to know that they can 'make a difference'. Could the Mallinson School be among those giving us all a lead?

As mentioned elsewhere, during that last visit while waiting in line at Delhi for the Srinagar flight, we found standing next to us a tall lady, conspicuous for her fair complexion. She turned to us, greeting me by name—our Old Girl, now a bank manager. Recognising her family name, I asked about her brother. She said, 'Oh, he was shot. He was one of a group of students.' Mrs Ray then met, in the course of that visit, women who had been little girls in the Mallinson Lower Primary Department during the five years she was running it, who are now doctors or lecturers. So, one is writing about a School which, like a family, is flesh and blood, suffering the sadnesses of our times, but also striving for the best for all.

9
THE HIPPIES: HOW THE IMAGE OF THE ENGLISHMAN CHANGED

What was it that attracted many Indians to the England they had never seen? Given the basic exploitation of any imperialism, given the racism of the Raj, the struggle for, and pride in, independence, there nevertheless entered into the hearts and minds of swathes of Indian society a deep attachment to many of the ways and the aspects of life that had been introduced by the British. This had surprised me when I first went to Pakistan in 1957. As an Englishman I was simply expected to be fair, truthful and wise. I started on a good wicket.

In my experience, at least until the seventies, the copying or retention of British ways was seen at different levels. The customs of the Officers' Mess in both India and Pakistan seemed frozen at about 1910. The humble government servant kept 'English time' and arrived at the office in perfectly creased trousers. At a deeper level there was the tradition of service and of honesty, sometimes more honoured in the breach than the observance, that was attributed, almost as a myth, to British times and especially to the Haileybury-bred ICS officers. This might often be focussed on a remembered relationship with a particular civil servant, soldier or missionary, or on the retelling of that memory from an even earlier time.

It is notable how the memory and the work of some of the best civil servants throughout colonial India has been valued and recorded in independent India. In the case of Kashmir it was the land settlement officer, Sir Walter Lawrence, whose work *The Valley of Kashmir* was republished in Srinagar as recently as 2011. Such men, many years ago, surveyed the fields, fixed a value and a rent, and did so without partiality or fear. People had known of a great and good ruler before— an Akbar—but the body of men who were the District Officers of the ICS between 1858 and 1947 left a mark of justice they had never associated with the powerful. If one reads the diaries or letters of men like Henry Lawrence or General John Malcolm one must credit their moral standing, for all their imperfections, to their faith. Their worldview was governed by the Enlightenment and by the astonishing reality of imperial rule, but their personal lives were lived in the light of their faith. To set the balance right, the foibles and follies of Simla society depicted by Kipling remind us that not all were saints, and that the saints were imperfect.

Thus, though many may not have grasped the source of the values of those 'English' (in reality often Ulstermen or Scots) who are now no more, they had in many ways assumed their ways. It was thus that their astonishment and shock at the arrival of the hippies was greater even than ours.

When we returned to Kashmir from UK leave in 1968 the School lawyer, Mr Shambunath Dhar, as always immaculate in his club blazer and RAF moustache, came to see me. 'Mr Ray, what *has* happened to England?' 'Plenty!' I said, 'why?' 'I saw an *Englishman, without shoes, begging,* in a *temple!*' At each word he paused for greater emphasis. He was deeply distressed. No amount of assurances that all Englishmen had not thus changed would comfort him. He felt that a linchpin had slipped from his world, and Mr Dhar, that archetype of the Hindu Englishman, was inconsolable. A little later the Governor of the State was helping to arrange the return to England of a hippy family who had got entangled in the coils of bureaucracy. Mr Bhagwan Sahai was no narrow nationalist, and would be the first to acknowledge the impracticality of his thought when he said to me, 'If I had my way I would stop all western literature coming into India!'

About the same time, I was travelling to Delhi by train with a lively crowd of students, medics and engineers from the Punjab. In one corner were two very dirty French hippies, tousled, sallow, smelling of *charas*. The students' animated conversation was partly for my benefit, and one finally turned to me and said, 'Sir, they shouldn't be allowed into India; they are spoiling our boys.'

We would see them all the time, those unconventional travellers, along the *bund* near Grindlay's Bank, sitting on the wall at Dal Gate, paddling *shikaras* or just lying in the warm waters of the Dal Lake, living in the cheap houseboats behind the willowy fringe in the backwaters. Those two, dirty and bedraggled, far gone, the urchins shouting after them and throwing stones … those others in saffron robes… Are these among them, parking their old Dormobile on the lakeside? Or those two I passed in the forest one morning, he fast asleep on a blanket quite naked, like a rather frail Greek god, she half in the sleeping bag?

To most Kashmiris they were simply the Hippies. To us they were a puzzle, an enigma, lightened by our experience of the few we came to know, as varied as human beings always are, yet telling us in total something significant about change in the West.

Eliza and Pierre came one pouring wet day in 1969. Was there anywhere they could stay for a night? Our place was as good as any, our children wide eyed, as they made themselves at home on our carpet. Eliza, daughter of a Seattle architect, willowy and fragile, had been sent by her parents to study art in Paris, and had stayed with Pierre's wealthy family. Pierre, strange and estranged, had been a leader in the 1968 student demonstrations and they had set off to the East together. After breakfast next morning they left for a villa above Nishat where some others were staying. Eliza said she would keep in touch, and we went out to see her a few days later. She was not feeling too good, and was breaking up with Pierre, who was not around. She had hepatitis and came back with us to stay. As she recovered she became a favourite with the children, gentle and loving. When she was well enough we sent her off—she was heading homewards, and was going to stay with friends on the way. Of Pierre we later heard that he had knocked at the door of the Mission Hospital at Manali, but had looked so wild and high that the girls there—the doctor was away—did not let him in. Much later we heard that Eliza and Pierre had met again, gone to Paris, married and have a family. So, some of these stories end well.

One morning I saw two ragged figures, one holding a child, sitting on the pavement to hitch a lift. I stopped and said they'd be more likely to get one a mile further out of town. Their accent spoke of the north-east of England, and we talked for a while. Later the girl, Doreen, had a second baby in a tent up at Pahalgam. Our friend Mairi, the doctor at the Mission Hospital at Anantnag, was camping nearby and offered Doreen the help needed, a small operation. Sometime later they went down the valley to the hospital where Doreen and the children were admitted while Alfred stayed along the road in the Hindu temple. They had both had a hard Newcastle upbringing, but Alfred was a graduate and had been a college lecturer. They had been married some years and had come eastwards in a Dormobile, which they had illegally sold in India, and thus could not leave the country. Mairi noticed the needle marks and found

Doreen not addicted and wanting to finish with drugs. From Anantnag they came on to stay with us. It was autumn and we were sleeping on the balcony. Alfred was in a dream world much of the time and the scent of marijuana wafted upward from their room, but Doreen was alive to the urgent needs of two ailing, squalling infants. They would go barefoot along the dirty *gulley* to the market, where all Kashmiris wore shoes. One day our five-year-old daughter said, 'You've forgotten your shoes.' 'Oh yes!' said Alfred and put them on.

It was October, the mornings were cold, and it was time for them to move on. The day they left was the day of my ordination as Deacon in the newly rebuilt church. They wished to come. Lakdasa de Mel from Sri Lanka, the Metropolitan, preached, and somehow the Spirit was present. The little family there, did they catch the 'good vibrations'? After lunch we took them out to the end of town, these two western refugees and their tiny children, a few coins all their wealth, to hitch a lift with all India before them.

Soon after this an American tourist called and asked if she could bring along a young couple staying in the next boat as she was worried about them. Next day Larry and Denise were at the door. Denise, a French-Canadian girl of nineteen, was pale and nervy but didn't look too bad. Larry, just eighteen and with an Ivy League accent, was white and thin to the bone, and shaking. They came in, our children watching open eyed as Larry opened on the carpet his small bag of pathetic possessions full of significance for him in his dream world: a crow's feather, an oddly shaped piece of wood, a stone, some paper, mouldering animal bones.

Denise told their story. Larry had set off eastwards some months earlier and was due to join his parents on their luxury yacht at Athens a few weeks hence. They had met up in Kabul, and Kashmir was to be the furthest point of their travels.

After staying in a cheap houseboat in Srinagar they had gone up to a camp in Pahalgam, a Shangri-La in the forest. No-one had told them that holiday makers in Pahalgam padlock and chain their possessions to the tent pole so that cases and valuables will not be eased out under the brailing by thieves working in gangs at night. Denise, whose money they were living off, had it stolen, and Larry lost his passport. Life took on a different aspect. In a place where truth was elusive, with no money or passport, who was he?

Our spare room was full, and we couldn't do much. What they needed was rest. I rang the Mother Superior at Baramulla … yes, they would take them. We packed them off on the bus. A few days later back they came: Larry still looked pale, but there was a new firmness in his handshake. 'The Lord found me,' he said. 'I sure was lost, and the Lord found me.' We marvelled. Somehow, between the clean sheets and the love of the nuns, and a vital word which Father Jim Borst had been able to speak, Larry had found and had been found. Denise also looked better, but perhaps negative experience from her school, a Quebec convent, had made too great a barrier, and she decided to move on. Larry stayed, but the lost passport was a problem. Father Borst suggested I contact the Superintendent of Police, who assured me that if it could be found, it would be found. We found Larry some better clothes and sent him off with a respected local friend to the DSP at Anantnag. He in turn sent him up to Pahalgam in a jeep with a police officer. Next evening when I came in, Catherine said, 'He's in there, asleep, and he's got his passport!' At Pahalgam they had searched everywhere. The servants of the hotel where they had stayed had been beaten to make them talk; all to no avail. Finally, the police officer had given up. 'We can't find it. We must type you out a form which will serve until you get to Delhi: but we have no typewriter at the police station.

What can we do?' Larry suggested they might have one at the bank. As they entered the manager looked up: 'Larry Jameson? Here is your passport!'

Larry had to get to Athens in two weeks to catch his parents on their luxury cruise. He wired them to send some money to Teheran and thought he could get that far cheaply in ten days. I lent him £25 and he set off. Sometime later Larry's mother wrote returning the money with thanks. She didn't really sound worried for her son. Months later we heard from Larry, now at an exclusive college in America. 'Here I am, forgetting and forgotten ... I still have my faith.'

When Denise and Larry had knocked at the door our spare room had been occupied by Jenny. A few weeks earlier I had received a telegram from the High Commission in Delhi saying, 'Please contact Lorna Haywood, British National aged 19, forcibly held on Houseboat 'Maid of the Mountains'. In the evening I walked up the river. There behind a screen of trees beyond the post office was the boat. Ignoring an invitation to come in I saw an English girl at the window. 'Lorna Haywood? I've had a telegram from Delhi. Come for a walk.' As we walked down the *bund* she told her story, so we went into the house and she told it again to Catherine, who said, 'You had better stay here.' With two Gurkha watchmen, not to be trifled with, and Gani the hostel cook, I retrieved her possessions from the boat. A few days later Lorna developed jaundice, so she had to stay on, becoming one more favourite aunt to the children while we got to know her well. Lorna's father was an engineer at Dounreay Atomic Station, a happy home but dull for a young girl; she was musical and a singer and had gone to Edinburgh, living with other young people .... a little hashish .... she didn't like it much. She had tried LSD and had seen a vision of Jesus on the cross while under its influence. Then she had set out eastwards, interested in Buddhism, in a ramshackle bus.

The bus had broken down at Delhi and five of the party had come up to Kashmir. Of these two had gone on to Australia, two had their money stolen and left, and Lorna, who was temporarily without money, had been invited by the houseboat owners into their own family boat. The romance and excitement of 'living with a real Kashmiri family' was only slowly lifting from her. How was she to know that no self-respecting Kashmiri would allow his daughter to stay alone on a boat? At first all had been well. Then slowly Lorna realised she was being tried out with suggestions. Perhaps—she had some experience of a handicrafts business in Scotland— hey could do some export business? Perhaps she could carry a little hashish? Was marriage the intention? A western bride could mean a hard currency bank account for the family. By now she was worried, but the eldest son, with his fluent English, smart clothes and good looks, rather impressed her. He went along to 'help' her at the bank when intimation of a money transfer from Scotland arrived. 'We're out of money just now; could you lend us the amount for a few days?' The young tend to believe the young, and Jenny parted with her money. She began to realise that she was in the family's power but was wise enough to keep the knowledge to herself. A German family came to stay on the adjoining tourist boat, and though warned against them and closely watched, she managed to make her plight known.

By this time she was being physically prevented by the women, arms akimbo, from leaving the boat, but before he left the German came on to the cook boat, and said to her in the hearing of the family, 'I will not take you to the airport as you don't have a ticket and would be sent back, but I shall tell friends in the British High Commission that you will arrive by next Monday: or if you do not, there will have been an accident.' Lorna became a friend, years later returning with her husband.

Not all our encounters ended happily. One day a houseboat man we knew came to the door. He asked us to come to his boat where a child was sick. The *shikara* took us across from Nehru Park to *Houseboat Ashram* (the names change with the times; older boats will be named *Prince of Wales* or *Gurkha*). In a small room was a German woman and her two children. She looked straight—not a hippy—though not conventional. Her older child, a red headed boy of about ten, was looking after her as well as he could. Her husband was away, and when we later saw him, he didn't look much use, both druggy himself and trading drugs, we thought. But her younger child, two and a half, was so thin that Catherine couldn't put the stethoscope on her corrugated ribs. She looked like an Oxfam poster baby. Whatever the original disease—it could have been typhoid—the child was desperately ill, starving and dehydrated.

We could talk only through an American boy, also living on the boat, who had jaundice, as only he spoke German and English well enough to interpret. We soon found that the mother had some deeply held unconventional beliefs and would only give 'macrobiotic' food. She had some maize flour in a jar, which she fed mixed with water. No sugar— she believed it would kill the child! Milk? It was almost unobtainable. Eggs, anything like meat or Bovril? These were 'very dangerous'. She mistrusted local homeopathic doctors, but 'chemical' medicine would kill the child. It was no use explaining that many western drugs are derived from natural products in controlled doses. She showed some interest in going to the Mission Hospital but learning that she would need to obey the doctor if she was admitted, and that a 'drip' might be needed, she declined. All we could do was to get some powdered milk to be mixed with the maize flour.

Two days later the boatman came again. The child was sinking, and we found her in a coma. The mother, realising that her much loved child was near death, was now willing for any treatment. We set off for the nearby State Hospital and hurried there, our own youngest child with us. On arrival the child was dead in its mother's arms. We could not even speak to try to comfort her.

There were many others: the American professor of philosophy so thin that he needed three hot water bottles as he was too cold to sleep, and his bones were aching. Our children said that he only ate tomatoes, but in fact he did eat fruit and vegetables—nothing else. There was Jan, the young Czech engineer, who had left Prague when the Russians came in and had lived in an ashram for a year before he had to escape over the wall at night. We last heard of him in a Christian meditation group in Paris.

In the sixties and seventies travel and life in India were cheap. Some came for spiritual experience, some to escape. *Cannabis indica* grew as a weed on the *bund* at the foot of our garden and could sometimes be seen along the roadside. It was said to be the mainstay of the parallel economy. When I asked our boys if any of their fathers smoked it, I received an offended and rather incredulous reply. Just occasionally the response was different; more in the eyes. It would not be surprising if one or two of their relatives traded in it.

The peak of the hippy trail to Kashmir passed. The Afghan war blocked the main route, and later travellers were usually better funded. Kashmir was expensive, cold for much of the year, and less welcoming than Goa, where (as we heard) tourists went 'to see the naked hippies'.

They had contributed to a lasting change in Kashmir's, and more widely in Muslim perceptions of the West, brought home to me at a School camp in 1985, when I overheard a parent, who had been visiting Newcastle upon Tyne, whose inner city I knew quite well, speaking of the 'white trash'.

Yet right up to 1986 Kashmir was a safe place where many thousands of young travellers had wonderful holidays. We tended to meet the casualties, but for the great majority, camping, trekking or lazing on a houseboat on Nagin or the Dal Lake, their stay in Kashmir was a high point in their journeys.

10
UNOFFICIAL REPRESENTATIVE

My appointment as Honorary Consul carried the title 'Unofficial Representative' because of the contested status of Kashmir. The role was to help British or Commonwealth nationals, both locally resident and visitors, who had problems; who fell sick, got lost, landed in prison or had died. As with the hippies we sought to help, some of the encounters were tragic, some more light hearted.

James Mackenzie, a very large man, arrived, newly deceased, by taxi at the front door. A partner in one of the Calcutta British firms, he had flown to Srinagar for a golfing holiday, gone straight up to Gulmarg at nine thousand feet, and promptly died of a heart attack. Without undertakers, burials had to be done by the small Christian community, and in the case of foreigners, that meant us. Phone calls revealed that the large body should be flown to Scotland. He was washed by Catherine and Mrs Chandra the School nurse and parked on ice in my study pending the arrival of a suitable coffin for air transport. A letter of thanks arrived ten days later from a familiar address in Stirlingshire, from someone I had taught at Gordonstoun, a close friend of Mr Mackenzie.

There was a happier outcome following a phone call from the High Commission in Delhi. Lord X, a household name and a member of the Jewish community, was very worried that his twenty-year-old daughter and two friends had disappeared while on holiday in Kashmir. Could she be traced? We had a parent in the local CID, the Foreigners'

Registration Department. Their duties included keeping files on people like me, but the wind blew both ways. They had no record of her, but this was not conclusive, as foreigners were checked at the airport, but not if travelling by road. The young lady was not a hippy, and would be staying with her friends, it was thought, in one of the medium or better-quality houseboats. Satara, the School Head peon, set off to enquire of the houseboats on the river, on the Dal Lake and on Nagin. No sign of her.

I told the High Commission that she didn't appear to be in Kashmir, but this only elicited a more urgent request, as Lord X was by now extremely worried. Satara redoubled his efforts, and had begun to search the small boats in the backwaters of the Lake, when a call came to say that she was safe. It transpired that she and her friends had changed their plans and had gone to the Kulu Valley instead of Kashmir. An apologetic letter followed, and a gift to a local good cause.

Prominent among resident British nationals were the Presentation Sisters at the Convent across the River Jhelum, and the Mill Hill fathers, our friends at Burn Hall School. Apparently in earlier days the CMS missionaries and their Roman Catholic counterparts scarcely acknowledged each other, but Vatican Two changed all that. Sister John, Sister Benedict and Sister Immaculata, rules relaxed for the first time, were now allowed to visit. They came to tea and delighted in our small children, then aged five, three and one. They themselves were as excited as children on a Sunday school picnic. They became good friends, as we steadily realised that what we shared was so much greater than what divided us. Several times when we had trouble outside the School in Lal Chowk one of the Sisters would telephone to say, 'We know what's happening your side of the River today Mr Ray. We're all praying for you!'

Father John MacMahon, an Edinburgh Scot, proved his friendship in many ways, so perhaps it is naughty to smile at the sad story of 'Father Eliot'. This began with a phone call from Burn Hall enquiring if we had met him. It was clearly our misfortune that we had not. The story was that Father Eliot, a priest of the Church of God, had been sent out of Uganda by Idi Amin, but had been able to take with him several Land Rovers, which were at Bombay. He wished to give them to worthy recipients, and the Catholic Hospital at Baramulla was to have one, and also Burnhall School. Day by day new details emerged. Visiting Burnhall, he saw one boy without a blazer, and on hearing that he was a poor teacher's son, money was produced on the spot. At Nedous Hotel his room was the centre of activity, with the whisky flowing and with well-tipped waiters hurrying back and forth. Father Eliot's home church was apparently in Manchester, known as 'The Little Gem'. His sister was in business there and had commissioned her brother to buy carpets in Kashmir. On the strength of a very large order Father Eliot had asked for and been given a cash advance of several thousand rupees by the carpet dealer.

Then we heard that next day one of the Baramulla Fathers was going to Bombay with their benefactor to drive the two Land Rovers back up to Kashmir, and that everyone was invited to a party at Nedous in the evening. We were impressed, but not quite convinced. At 7 pm Monseigneur and everyone else duly assembled with the hotel manager. 7.15 came, and ....7.30, but no Father Eliot. Then down in the office the clerk recalled that a taxi driver had asked him to phone his wife, saying that he had a fare to Jammu and wouldn't be back till next day. One phone call to the police at Batote, and a few hours later a disconsolate Father Elliot was back, this time in the cells at Kothi Bagh. There is only one mountain road out of Kashmir.

His cassock, it turned out, had been stolen from the Anglican church in Simla. I met him next day in his cell, shaking from DTs. He had no passport, but at police request I asked the High Commission in Delhi if he could be given papers and a one-way ticket to the UK. The High Commission told me that he had already been flown back to Britain from Brazil and from Israel under different names, and had been in jail in Madras and elsewhere in India. They didn't want to know. The local police took him to the State border at Kathua and set him loose. The next spring Father MacMahon reported that he had seen him on the steps of the Catholic Bishops' Centre in Delhi. We heard no more.

Very different was the story of Alison. A call from the High Commission in Delhi informed us that a Mr MacDonald and a Mr Merry were coming from Britain after learning that Ken MacDonald's daughter Alison had disappeared in Kashmir. Alison and her friend Liz, students at Aberdeen University, had come to Kashmir on holiday, stayed in a houseboat and gone to Sonamarg. Liz had gone off trekking for four days leaving Alison in the Glacier Hotel—little more than a hut at that time—until she returned, when they planned to go on by bus over the Zoji La to Ladakh.

When Liz returned she found that Alison had vanished four days earlier. The hotel owner said that the room was paid for, and he presumed that she had also gone off trekking. Liz raised the alarm and contacted her father in Surrey who, with Alison's father, flew straight out.

The MacDonalds are no ordinary family. Kenny had been with Customs and Excise for twenty years and had played amateur football for Scotland. In 1981 he had started to train for the ministry of the Free Church. The family had lived on the rugged island of Skye and it was clear that Alison would not have fallen into a river or run into danger carelessly. She and Liz were both judo enthusiasts. As we were to discover, the MacDonalds are a strongly united family, and notes found in Alison's bible showed her to have been a firm Christian. She would not have gone off, hippy style. Liz's father had connections with Mr B K Nehru, the Governor of Kashmir State, and through him the High Altitude Warfare School at Sonamarg, and the State Police were involved.

Kenny and Reta followed up every possible lead and visited Kashmir eight times in all over a period of three years, often staying in our house as a base. For a long while it seemed as if Alison was just beyond our sight. Prolonged searches led to the conclusion that she had been kidnapped and spirited out of the State. Is she today a wife and mother in Arabia or elsewhere? The book *Alison: A Father's Search for His Missing Daughter* gives a vivid picture of the Kashmir scene as well as a moving account of an extraordinary search. In 1983, following information that finally proved false, Kenny went from the Pakistan side, again with co-operation from the military at high level, right up to the cease-fire line in the Gurais sector. There has been no word, no real clue, in all these years. Seeing the wonderful faith of the family, it is impossible to view the matter as unrelieved tragedy: but mystery it remains.

The overseas community in Srinagar was very small, its largest component being among the staff of the Convent or Burn Hall, who were in any event close friends. During the Pakistan wars of 1965 and 1971 we were asked by the British High Commission to arrange a bus for any British nationals who might wish to leave; but in the event, none wanted to go.

One never knew who would come walking across to our pleasant home. Usually it was to ask a little help or advice. Sometimes it was tragedy, as when a young woman came to say that her trekking partner had been swept away in front of her eyes by the Zanskar River, far from help or habitation. On another occasion we were caught up in a disaster on the Zoji La. A trekking party and their porters, unable to get a bus from Kargil in time to catch their flight, had crowded onto a truck for Srinagar; some up in the crow's nest above the cab, a whole crowd in the back and at least two in the cab. High on the pass the brakes failed, and the truck somersaulted down over a thousand feet, tossing people into the air and crushing others. We were involved in burials, in visiting the injured in hospital and caring for the porters in the school hostel; also, in meeting next of kin who travelled from Europe to find out what had happened. One single young man was thrown out unhurt and managed to get on his booked flight straight back to his London office.

Two weeks later Christina, a young German woman, strange and estranged, appeared in my School office. Her parents had just divorced and her mother I had just buried. She was a member of a far-left group active at that time, utterly distressed as she poured out her angry story, staying in our home for a few days. Like much else in Kashmir, there was an extra twist to the story. The police had simply given me four coffins, sealed up and with name tags affixed. One was of a young Dutch boy, another of an Anglo-Indian young man from Himachal, whose family also came to Srinagar and wanted their son's coffin opened. When this was done, it was seen to contain not their son but the fair-haired young Dutchman. Moreover, we then found that the bodies had not been washed, and were still as when recovered on that bleak mountainside.

Normally, wishing to avoid any possible political involvement, I only represented Commonwealth nationals. One day, just after the School had been closed following some 'trouble', a Japanese tourist walked into my office and told me that his Australian friend had accidentally got caught up in a riot and been killed. He said that his body had been set on fire and the police had quietly buried him. This was rather sensitive, but an Australian consular official came up and recovered the dead person's belongings.

Lest this sounds like a litany of disasters it's good to remember the great numbers of tourists from across the world who trekked in the mountains or stayed in houseboats in the seventies and eighties, when war and terror seemed far away. On Nagin or the Dal, visiting Gulmarg, Pahalgam and Sonamarg or shopping at Suffering Moses or Asia Crafts, thousands, as well as far greater numbers of Indian visitors, enjoyed safe and memorable holidays in that most beautiful of valleys: the Valley of Kashmir as we will always recall it.

We were there long enough to see the world from a central Asian as well as from a British perspective. At the street level we felt the stirrings of religious radicalism. British support for Gulbuddin Hekmatyar, most extreme of the mujahedeen, seemed to me short-sighted and perverse. Aware of these dynamics, I wrote to Mrs Thatcher warning that they would not go away after defeating the Russians but would come back to bite us. I received no reply.

11
FOUR HOUSEMASTERS

The Senior School had four houses, each named after a Kashmir mountain climbed on a few or many occasions by School parties, and each with the name of a beautiful Kashmir bird as its totem. Thus, we had Tatakuti, Kolahoi, Mahadev and Haramukh houses, represented by the Paradise Flycatcher, the Golden Oriole, the Blue Kingfisher and the Hoopoe as their totems. In the sixties we would catch glimpses of all these birds.

For ten years until 1972 Mr Salamuddin was Vice Principal and masters Sat Lal Razdan, Balji Saproo, Amarnath Mattoo and Kashinath Dhar were the four housemasters. In the Junior School Mr Radhakishen Kaw was the Head, and from 1965 Miss Margaret Shaw ran the Lower Primary School. These made up my kitchen cabinet, without whose sometimes critical but always significant support the School would have failed. All except Miss Shaw were Old Boys, and she had started her schooling in Mary Grove's wartime school at Gulmarg. There was one more: Mr Arjan Nath Mujoo the Bursar, greatly loyal and, of course. an Old Boy.

Pir Salamuddin lived just across old Amirakadal bridge in Maisuma. His green *pagri* was a passport to most homes in the City, and at times of tension his status was a safeguard to us. A *Pir* may have many roles, but with Mr Salamuddin, at least as far as the School was concerned, it was primarily as a man of wisdom and good advice. I hope the little Central Asian-style mosque behind his home still stands, but whatever his role there, with us, in Sheikh Bagh, in camp at Sang i Sufaid or Nichinai, on the Dal Lake or on Mahadev he was always at the heart of the party, alert and decisive. Not a man of many words—not ones I could understand anyway—his discipline was sharp, his comments pithy and his warnings to be taken seriously.

It was the four housemasters, all Old Boys, who remained the core of the staff throughout my quarter century. They were also all Kashmiri *Pandits*, representatives like Jawaharlal Nehru of a unique and precious community. It is a commentary on our age that none of their children live today in Kashmir. Sat Lal's son, with whom he lived until his death in Jammu, is a widely acclaimed neurologist. Balji Saproo's and Amarnath's sons are in Delhi, and Kashinath's boy went to Bombay as an engineer in the Naval Dockyard. But I remember them as a band of brothers, equally at home in the busyness of the School, or wearing shorts and carrying a rucksack in the high and beautiful straths among the mountains.

Mr Sat Lal one remembers as more than a housemaster, but even as Head of the Senior School and Vice Principal, he still cried out in his high-pitched voice, 'Come on, Tatakuti!' He stood out as a remarkable human being, rather apart from the others. For a start, he came from Anantnag, thirty-four miles distant and with a different accent, not a city dweller. Educated in the CMS School there, he was picked out by Dr Edmonds when that school was handed to government. Phil saw his leadership qualities which he helped to develop. In 1963, when my ties with the British Council were still fresh, I was able to send him with their help for a term to Gordonstoun.

As Head of Science his labs were always busy, and the practicals were never missed. He was an enthusiast and enthused others, many of whom went on to science-based careers. After the 1965 fire he went himself to Ambala to ensure the best new equipment was obtained. Whatever happened—fire, flood, war with Pakistan, whatever—Sat Lal would always be in the lead, jumping into a *nallah* to help the smallest boys across, urging on his house whether on the sports field or at the Sinking the Boat race, always urging them to be and to do their best. He was proud to see his son, Sushil, go on to excel in medicine, but equally proud that his daughter became an engineer, not a common role for a girl in those days.

Sat Lal Razdan was widely honoured as an outstanding teacher. His book *Spirit and Science*, typically dedicated to 'my dear fellow teachers and dear old boys and old girls,' reflects his own human and catholic spirit, embracing everyone. It also reflects both his deep enthusiasm for science and his reflective, philosophical and religious nature. It contains his poems 'And we lament at what has happened' and 'Dear Kashmiris'. These remind us that he, like his whole remarkable community, are refugees, yet speak with a confidence that the mutual affection of Kashmiris for one another would finally triumph. I found myself kept up to the mark by Sat Lal. A last minuter, if I should be one minute late he would be looking at his watch, saying, 'English time, Mr Ray!'

Mr Balji Saproo, Kolahoi Housemaster and Head of Maths, was the conscience of us all. Calm, wise and deeply sincere, he commanded the respect of boys and staff alike and thus never needed to raise his voice. Earlier in life, it was said, he had been influenced by the Moral Re-Armament movement. Balji looked after the Poor Fund with great seriousness, scrupulously keeping the accounts of the quite large sums of money given, form by form. He would regularly accompany boys to visit the homes of widows and others in need, and organised our annual visits to Yaqub Shah and the Leper Colony with great care, seeing that we had the supplies and medicines most needed. His home at the far end of the city, was like most *Pandit* homes conservative in its rituals, and it is thus a memory of special privilege that Mrs Ray and I enjoyed the most delicious vegetarian feast there.

There can often be a tendency to agree with the latest designs, not always well thought through, of the person in charge. In Kashmir it is called *makhan*—butter, or flattery. When all others agreed, if Mr Balji gently suggested that I pause and think the matter through, I came to realise that I should indeed do so.

Very different in personality, though also of great value to the School, was Mr Amarnath Mattoo. He was Housemaster of Mahadev House and Head of Social Sciences, a geographer who had travelled the world. He also had a role in the maintenance of our estate, perhaps best illustrated by a story. Sir John Lawrence, a descendant of the nineteenth-century Lawrences of the Punjab, was staying for a few days, I think amazed at the smooth functioning of our large City centre undertaking. 'Who is your fixer?' he asked. I replied, trying to take the moral high ground, 'We don't have a fixer!' Then I thought, yes, the sagacious Mr Amarnath is the one who can mollify, enlist, enable progress against every bureaucratic or personality-fuelled obstacle.

Last but not at all least of the four was Mr Kashinath Dhar, Haramukh Housemaster, Head of English, in charge of cricket and a stylish batsman, a keen gardener and good neighbour in his Muslim neighbourhood. Kashinath was a heart and soul enthusiast for our expeditions, camps and swims, as indeed were the others, but he would often be foremost in any undertaking. He could be quick tempered, but usually with ample cause. Like the rest, he would fight his corner—usually for his House. A very honest person, he would bluntly tell a truth where others might temporise. On one occasion, cycling out to a regatta at Nehru Park I said to him, 'Kashinath, everyone here takes and gives bribes. Do our Old Boys, just like the rest?' He thought over this serious matter, then said, 'Yes, everyone here takes bribes. Our Old Boys do too.' Then after a pause added, 'But they know it's wrong..' Kashinath was a greatly loved and valued member of our team. When this story was retailed to Dick Lucas, the Rector of a leading City church, he commented. 'Ah yes, the Old Testament before the New!'

It was men like these who set the tone for everyone. With up to two hundred boys in the water on Dal Cross day it was only their extraordinary level of watchfulness that kept us free of accidents.

Few of our less senior *Pandit* staff could look back to their childhood moulding in the School in the same way, though many who had not that advantage contributed notably. Almost overnight in 1989 they left, never to return. Several found employment in our sister school in Jammu, where the Principal has long been Esther William, Bishop Aziz's daughter.

The School was also enriched by teachers from the far corners of India and beyond, and by the short-termers, often gifted eighteen-year-olds. The last of the overseas missionaries, Alan and Rosemary Nickless, and Cynthia Morgan, who is laid to rest in the cemetery beside the School, blessed us by their notable service. Is it fanciful to see the start and finish of that enterprise as having cost two very special lives? Miss Morgan, as many parents and pupils of hers will remember, was a person who gave everything. Dr Elmslie, whose medical help to the Maharajah as well as to many poor Kashmiris, had paved the way for permission for foreigners to stay in Kashmir through the winter, had died at Gujarat in Punjab after contracting pneumonia crossing the

Pir Panjal Pass in a snowstorm in October 1871. Wanting to help for as long as possible he had left the Valley too late.

I have highlighted 'Four Housemasters' and the Kashmiri *Pandit* community in this passage. It was some members of the non-Old Boy staff of the same community who gave me headaches during the tussles that led to the 1973 strike. I sympathised with them but could not be ruled by them. It had to be put to a very public testing. As it turned out the parents, old students and government shared my view and that of our management. It should be added that most of these younger *Pandit* staff also gave very valuable service.

But this is a celebration of the people and the memories of a less complicated time, when we were unchallenged in our determination to put boys of differing religions and cultures together in each tent, each boat. Whatever our occasional differences, memory retains the good and grace causes us to forget the imperfect. We were a band of brothers.

12
THE HOSTEL

The iconic building still stands. Over a century old, it looks out across the main field to Residency Road but has been without its stalwart squad of boys from Leh and Kargil for nearly thirty years. Throughout our time it was an essential feature of the School. Mr and Mrs Chandra Pandit were almost as iconic as the building. Chandra, one of the small number of Christians from that community, and Judith his Punjabi wife, the School Nurse, were the guardians of this fortress, and in times of trouble could set their boys to work, day or night. It was they who had seen the flames when the main block was on fire one night in March 1965 and had dived under burning rafters into the office to rescue School records and furniture and to get to the telephone to call the fire brigade.

In grounds so exposed to intruders it was vital to have such a force close at hand. Mrs Chandra was there for anyone in need, such as the occasion during a fracas on the road front when a villager was severely beaten by police, having found himself caught up in a mob of whose concerns he was totally ignorant. When encroachments were attempted on any of our boundaries, usually at night, Chandra's ears and eyes were our first line of defence.

A spare room on the top floor was always there for travellers or groups needing basic accommodation, provided they passed Chandra's vetting. Batchelor staff from Kerala or elsewhere beyond the Kashmir Valley made it their home, and the British short-termers both gave and received much through their stay there. But it was the boys who gave the place its distinctive family feel, the older ones caring for the smaller children. Buddhist, Muslim and Christian: the Ladakhi identity was distinctive, their mutual support notable, their reliability and good behaviour the norm. The food like the accommodation, was adequate but basic.

Coming from areas inaccessible in winter, when Srinagar was also cold and unwelcoming, from New Year the whole Hostel family migrated to Gurdaspur in Punjab, where some old mission buildings were available. They went by bus, two days' journey, but one year I suggested a few might cycle there. Just three were up for it, Phuntzog Kalon and two others, and I decided to go with them as far as Jammu, a hundred and seventy mountain miles, stopping overnight with friends at Batote. The weather was cold, with snow beside the road as we set off up the Valley. The climb from Khanabal towards the Banihal tunnel was hard work for heavy bikes with no gears and I noted that the boys were apprehensive as we climbed slowly between banks of snow. Fortunately, there was no convoy in the tunnel and as we sped down the south-facing slopes the mood lightened. 'The Kashmiris said we'd die in the tunnel, but we didn't!' exclaimed Phuntzog. The road, mainly downhill but running over forbidding drops, led us past the well-named Khuni Nallah to the Chenab crossing at Ramban, where we were faced with a steady climb of four thousand feet. An Ambassador car overtook us as we toiled up the road then stopped just ahead. 'Mr Ray, can I help you?' was the kind but uncomprehending query from a parent who appeared to think me unable to afford any easier transport. The next day's journey was over Patni Top and on through Udhampur to Jammu into warmer weather. After staying there with our Chairman, Bishop Aziz William, the boys cycled on into Punjab while next day I put my bike on a bus for the return to Srinagar.

Friday night was Hostel night for me. Going in by the kitchen door one was greeted by Gani, Hostel cook. Massive, totally reliable and valued for his good sense, good humour and sure control of the boys, he would be preparing to serve dinner to twenty or more lads, a VSO or other short-termer, and Mr and Mrs Chandra, Warden, School Nurse and Matriarch. There might also be one or two visitors staying in one of the top floor rooms. Gani had a helper, usually a poor young man who did most of the preparation and cleaned the pots.

The menu was unchanging but hungry boys don't worry about variety. At the summons they would file up with their tin plates for rice, curried *sag*, *aloo* or other vegetables and—the Friday night special—two chunks of meat. Grace said, silence fell. The curried mutton pieces would be left at the side until last, then to be savoured at leisure.

Beyond the two long tables one piece of furniture dominated: a full-size ping pong table. I was always challenged. The boys were pretty good. I sometimes won one game in three, but hardly ever won two. Honourably beaten I would be treated to a dazzling display by the reigning champions.

Conversation, so far as memory serves, was general, perhaps about 'the road': whether the Zoji La was closed by landslide or snow, perhaps about things going on in School or in the City. The kitchen entrance was often left open. Seva Singh the Gurkha Chowkidar would look in on his rounds. The seat beside the stove was attractive in winter. A visiting parent might arrive off a late bus or even, with Chandra Pandit's permission, be staying for the night. Talk was unconstrained, guided by Ladakhi good humour. The boys from Leh were mainly Buddhist, with one or two Christians, while the Kargilis were usually Muslim.

Chandra Pandit and Judith had a final say, and it would be a brave boy who challenged their rule; but generally, the atmosphere was relaxed and cordial. Chandra might need me to sign a cheque or have something to discuss. Gani might have a word of wisdom as I passed into the darkness by the kitchen door.

The Chandras finally retired to the house they had built at Chanapora and passed the care of the Hostel to Mr and Mrs Nickless. Of their own children, Vijay was one of the first ski instructors at Gulmarg while Vinu, who worked in the HMT watch factory for many years, is Associate Priest at All Saints Church.

13

CONTRASTS

Cloudburst: *This excerpt from the Tyndale Biscoe Centenary Souvenir of 1980 gives something of the flavour of many good days.*

Senior Camp had been successful in spite of a lot of rain. The boys had gone to Tarsar, to the foot of the Kolahoi glacier, to Tulyan, and they left Pahalgam for home in the buses that brought 290 twelve- to fourteen-year-olds. With them came the sun; the Third Plateau rang with their enthusiasm, whether at Tent Inspection, at Games, preparing for Camp Fire or on Trek. Each house had a two-day trek. The first day they had to walk thirteen miles and climb 3.000 feet to the meadow at Armiun, under Kolahoi, where tents were ready pitched. Next day they climbed over Korapather at 11,660 feet and returned to Camp by the East Lidder. I accompanied the seventy-four boys of the last party, Mahadev House. At 8.15 am the long line was checked for raincoats and everyone set off for the track to Aru, which was reached in good order by 11.30 am. We set off after a rest and stopped for lunch from *tiffin carriers* a few hundred feet up at the edge of the forest. From here on the path was narrower, steeper, running between the torrent of a river below and the steep cliffs above. Twice we crossed the river by wooden bridges; only occasional *gujars* were seen. At last, at 4pm, we topped a rise and there, across a beautiful meadow, were the tents beside a sparkling river. Tiredness forgotten, all broke into a run. Five minutes later the line was taking tea and *chapatis* from Gani and Ismaila, and Master Waqil was giving out blankets. For two hours the boys played; some even swam in the glacier river. Then the rain came. Thunder, heavy rain, and then a cloudburst. I looked round to see rivers of chocolate rushing through the boys' tents. They stood up in the tents in their blankets while the water poured over their ankles, the tent floor a lake. For twenty rather frightening minutes the sky was rent by lightning, our ears were full of thunder, and of the furious noise of the downpour, and we could only stand and wait for a lull. Then suddenly it ended, and we inspected. One 'river' had doused the kitchen fire: the tents were hopeless. Vakil and I went to see the *gujar*. The *numbardar* offered to take all seventy boys in his hut, so after supper—cold meat, curry and rice—the party trooped across there.

They all slept and the *gujar*'s wife, a kind and resourceful woman, kept her *chulha* ablaze all night for the boys, who must have gained a new picture of *gujar* life. Next morning the sky was blue, and the river had fallen to its usual size. The scene was idyllic as the sun crept over the mountains in the early morning, and the children were reluctant to leave—threading in a line up between the birch trees to the pass above, looking down on our tents and beyond to the glacier, Buttress Peak, and a glimpse of Kolahoi summit.

What a trip for twelve-year-olds! Not one complained, not one fell sick. How much the poorer we would have been without that storm, and the experience it brought.

Teargas

I hesitate to include this: the Kashmir experience has been so deeply traumatic and tragic for so many and for so long, that this seems almost like an intrusion into a grieving. Yet it was a small foretaste, a part of our common experience in those years, and as such should perhaps be recorded.

We usually had some warning. Maybe the SP College students were upset about one thing or another. Or maybe it was something political. Or rent-a-mob had been at work. On one occasion the latter was paid, said our staff, by a local Congress Party worker raising anger against his own party's decision in Delhi to cut the rice subsidy to Kashmiris. That decision was duly reversed the next day. If Gani or Satara, head servants with their ears to the ground, said, 'It's the public', it meant something big.

Anyway, they usually came down Residency Road, whether to demonstrate in Lal Chowk or to cross the river towards the Secretariat. The police, or if it was really serious the Kashmir Armed Police or the Border Security Force, wanted to stop them getting into Lal Chowk. That meant at the School gate.

I can't remember whether it was ten or twenty occasions in those normally peaceful years, but we developed a simple drill, and everyone knew what to do. Our aim was always to keep out both the rioters and the police, as if one lot came in the other was likely to follow. On one occasion when the police were thin on the ground we saw a constable jump over the fence and remove his uniform. The first sign of imminent trouble was the shops closing; their shutters coming down. The street vendors moved away, and local buses would hurry into the stand opposite. We would send a word round that the bell would not ring for change over, break or lunch. The message would be passed to the Lower Primary and the Girls' School, farther back from the road. The main gate was shut, and the small one guarded. Parents or servants might hurry in to collect a child and leave by one of the rear entrances. Classes in the main Senior School block on the

roadside would be kept away from the windows. We were not usually the target, but often lost a few window panes from flying stones.

The traffic had stopped, and everything went quiet. The police were massed across the road and in the bays where the buses pulled in. As the crowd approached, often with some flag bearers, a whistle was blown, followed by the popping of tear gas and often the confusion of a *lathi* charge, shouts and cries. We kept out of sight, well back behind the stout fence. The teargas might be repeated for some time and drifted across into the School. The demonstrators would finally scatter or regroup. What we had seen might be isolated or it might be part of something bigger across the City. A curfew might be imposed, and life shut down, perhaps until Friday prayers had passed. On a few occasions there would be police shooting to disperse the mob, maybe with one or two killed, but up to the time we left in October 1986, this was rare.

Whatever the further outcome there was usually a pause after the initial police confrontation. The older children would leave, often taking little ones with them. Brothers would collect sisters from the Girls' School. Relatives and servants collected many. By late afternoon there might be just a few still waiting. No cell phones in those days, but the School phones rang constantly. The staff, themselves anxious, would wait until everyone had left.

The smell of teargas hangs around, and I would walk back across our quiet and peaceful grounds with a lingering headache. Next day and perhaps until the following week School would be off. We never lost a child in all those years. On the few occasions when we had our roadside windows pelted I would always get them replaced at once. A parent who was also a neighbour once asked me why I kept on repairing the glass. He smiled at my reply, 'Because I have faith in Indian democracy.'

'The Mourning After'

This was the heading in *The Indian Express*, referring to the official mourning after the death of Jagjivan Ram, an aged politician. 'Holidays as part of official mourning are invariably a windfall for a class of people already pampered with a sufficient number of off days. And it is even more absurd to close schools, where students generally have a less than abiding interest in the passing of politicians.'

Our School had Muslim holidays as most of the boys are Muslim. Hindu holidays are necessary as Kashmiri *Pandits* were well represented. We had one Sikh and one Buddhist holiday and, as we are a Christian school, Christian holidays. When government is weak and wants to please people, rather minor Muslim saints' days are also proclaimed holidays. All this is apart from 'holidays' declared when violence is likely or has occurred.

But the most essential holidays are those decreed as a mark of respect for the dead. Keen not to waste precious school time I resisted these for years. But woe to the foreign Head who fails to observe a national hero's passing! Imagine then my surprise when *two* days of national mourning were declared, with all schools and government offices closed the length and breadth of India, on the assassination of Lord Mountbatten.

The most mourned passing was that of Jai Prakash Narayan, last of the genuinely great Ghandians. He was on the brink for days, then one lunchtime Mr Misri hurried across to the house with the news that he was dead. For such a person immediate closure was in order, no matter how difficult for the infants' department. A special assembly was called at the start of afternoon school. I said my piece and had just asked for a minute's silence as a mark of respect when, 'psst! psst!' from Mr Misri. 'What is it?' I whispered. 'He's not dead!' came the voice. We managed to dissolve the assembly decently and returned to classes. We were, of course, not alone. The national parliament had beaten us by a few minutes and had closed before the news came that Mr Narayan was, in fact, still living. He could die peacefully a few weeks later.

Fire!

The older Kashmiri houses are timber framed, floored and roofed. The City houses, higgledy-piggledy, festooned with telegraph and electricity wires and poles, face their greatest danger from fire. Even the traditional *kangri*, taken to bed and sometimes upset under the *razai*, is a great fire raiser. Canon Biscoe vividly recounts how, when fire and terror struck, the people in desperation would throw their belongings from the upper stories into the streets, only for neighbours to loot whatever was saved. Thus, he set up and trained masters to operate the School fire pump, the origin of Srinagar's modern fire service.

Given the nature of Srinagar society, there are reasons other than closely packed wooden buildings for fires. Hope of insurance, fear of audit, enmity, or desire to create panic are just a few of them. Soon after we arrived in 1962, a chimney fire developed in the Canon's old house in which we had a flat. Eric Biscoe summoned the fire brigade, and by the time it arrived, a lot of smoke was belching up. Were the beams abutting the chimney stack catching fire? The crew took their time, leisurely unrolling hoses, standing around as the smoke increased. They then sat down to watch while Eric fumed. Fortunately, Gili Bakshi, a boy in the School whose uncle was Chief Minister, saw the situation. 'Come on. Get your hoses working. You won't get any money here!' The fire was reluctantly put out, but one can imagine … at times a lot of *baksheesh* must be paid; the longer the delay, the higher the payment.

As mentioned elsewhere, in March 1965, while in the Red Sea returning from UK leave aboard RMS *Caledonia*—how beautiful those ships were!—we were handed a cable as we went in to dinner: SCHOOL BURNED DOWN RETURN IMMEDIATELY.' Fortunately we were eastbound, so I flew from Aden leaving Catherine and *Caledonia* to continue at twenty knots via Karachi to Bombay. I arrived to see the High School building on the roadside largely burned out, presenting a miserable sight, with March floodwater standing in the field and some tents erected in dry patches for classes to continue. Remarkably not a day had been lost, with classes continuing in spare space in the Hostel and even the garage.

'Your first job is to get the School servants out of Sher Garhi Police Station', said Mr Salamuddin. Sure enough, there they all were, with a grubby blanket apiece, sharing a damp, straw floored cell. They were glad to see me, each in turn showing the cigarette burn marks, mainly on the neck; a minor torture designed to extract a 'confession'. I got them out, and it was clear enough they had nothing to confess. The police finding, which helped us from the insurance aspect, was that the fire was accidental, starting from charcoal which the servants had left in a bucket under a wooden staircase.

There had been a similar accidental fire when the Convent had gone up in flames, another the night after ours at a large building just across the road, and yet another on the road to the airport.

Sometimes there was no guessing—the arson is obvious. One of the City's distinguished buildings was the Raj Garh, the Old Palace of the Dogra Maharajahs. After 1947 it had served as the meeting place of the State Assembly, and although *bukhari* smoke had spoiled many of the fine papier-mâché ceilings, the palace, close to Badshah Bridge on the River Jhelum, still had charm and dignity. In

1983 there were headlines in the Delhi papers of a crisis in Kashmir, while in Srinagar nothing appeared amiss. It seemed that some in Delhi wanted the end of Farooq Abdullah's government, that the Speaker had changed sides, and that it would be put to the test in the Assembly the next day. After school we saw the column of smoke and walked along the *bund* to join the large crowd on Amirakadal Bridge. We watched silently as flames leapt out of windows, roofing fell in, and part of the Palace slipped into the river, sizzling and steaming as it went. No anger or surprise appeared. The impassive crowd understood to a man that persons unknown wanted the building burnt.

In the 1970s there was the 'Pandit Agitation' following the elopement of a Brahmin girl with a Muslim youth (as it was rumoured). Suddenly there was a widespread outbreak of mysterious fires. Two of our staff had their homes set on fire. Everyone feared the unknown fire raisers. It was said that seventy-five rupees was the going rate for starting a fire, but who was paying and who received it never became clear. Two English tourists had asked me to suggest a day's trek off the beaten track, so I had sketched out a route over a forested spur to the village of Pastun, from where they could get to Tral and a bus back to Srinagar. As the pair came down out of the forest into Pastun, their way was barred by a crowd of villagers, armed with axes, clubs and iron bars, ready to defend their homes against the unknown fire raisers. Knowing no Kashmiri, they were taken to the village schoolmaster, who understood some English and proclaimed them harmless. The same week I met a shaken Mr Dar, Deputy Director of Education, just returning in his jeep from a visit to another village. Smoothing his hair, he told me breathlessly that he had only just escaped with his life from a similar crowd and, unable to persuade them, was glad to have got back safely to Srinagar.

To bring this section more up to date, the Principal of St Paul's School, showing us the fire damaged but just functioning school after the arson of 2010 said to us, 'Our family are used to fires!' She was referring to Pastor Yonathan's home, the All Saints Church House, torched by mobs who had set fire to All Saints Church in 1967 and 1979.

After all, there is the Kashmiri saying, 'If your house is burned down you rebuild it a storey higher.'

Maps

Our artist friend Jyoti Sahi was arrested as he completed a sketch of the landscape in Kashmir which included a bridge. If I had produced a map the same would quickly have resulted. I kept my inherited maps tucked away and did small sketches of any new route I was planning. By the time we left Srinagar in 1986 I probably knew the remote corners of the Valley better than any non-Kashmiri. At Camp and High Camp each summer we took small and large parties of boys across wild and untrodden places; over peaks, passes and snow beds, fording rivers, crossing snow bridges, finding the way where no path existed.

In term time week by week a class of boys would get to School by about 7 am to pile into the back of a bus going to some remote destination. We explored together not the beauty spots advertised to tourists but the forest paths, hill passes and hamlets where visitors were unknown. We also visited remote ancient sites, the remains of temples, palaces and canals from the eighth-century Hindu kingdom. Without prior detailed sketches much of our exploring could not have happened.

Maps have been my favourite reading since my early teens, when I began to explore England by bicycle. It was wartime, and every road sign, even ancient milestones, had been removed lest they should guide the enemy in the event of invasion. Much of my exploration of the countryside was guided by the Bartholomew's pocket atlas that would fit in my back pocket, or by the survey maps which showed every farmhouse, stream or footpath. The ancient castles, churches and villages were a delight awaiting exploration. The place names spoke of a history going back over a thousand years, and meeting country people introduced one to a land still largely unchanged by modernity. Even places I never visited remain strong in imagination. One might ponder who, or what, were Saint Endellion, Margaret Roding or Cheddon Fitzpaine? The great open downlands, with their even more ancient stone circles and burial mounds, took one back four thousand years into pre-history.

From the age of eighteen, at university when the Scottish mountains became my passion, it was the Ordinance Survey maps, in those days an inch to a mile, which were one's sure safeguard. In mist, white-out or blizzard to read off and then to follow the bearing could be the difference between safety and disaster. Descending from the summit of Ben Nevis often in cloud and snow and seeking the shelter of the climbers' hut, a bearing of a hundred and thirty-five degrees from the summit, down the darkening slopes, led the party between precipitous invisible cliffs to the left, and tempting but illusory openings to the right. Then finally the ridge narrowed to a point where one could safely descend.

It was in Kashmir that I encountered those mar vels of cartography, the beautiful and incredibly accurate maps of the nineteenth-century exploration of the Himalaya by the Survey of India. Every remote bend of each mountain torrent, footpath or collection of *gujar* huts had been faithfully recorded over vast areas, far from any road, where the surveyors had travelled by mule or pony with theodolite and all their baggage, doing a work of extraordinary accuracy.

Miss Mallinson, MBE, who had in her own words 'come to be with the women of Kashmir when they needed help' in 1924, and had stayed for nearly forty years, had by 1947 become the residuary legatee of the maps left to her by the Biscoes, the Neves, the Hadows and other British families who had loved the people and the landscape of Kashmir, to which the 'half inch' sheets of the Survey had been the key.

She left over a hundred of those maps, one inch, half inch and quarter inch sheets, to me. I soon learned that it was unwise to be seen with one: perhaps one was a spy or a Pakistani agent? For our quarter century in Srinagar they stayed in an old trunk. I made careful notes and sketch plans of routes where I planned to take parties of boys on class expeditions, often finding forest paths which led from one valley to another—from Khrew to Harwan or from Woyil over Mohan Marg to the Erin Nallah and Bandipore. The small paths, used by villagers or *bakarwals* from time immemorial remained just as they had been trodden and faithfully documented by the surveyors of a century earlier.

Our link with these extraordinary map makers was Colonel Phillimore, for long Deputy Surveyor General of India. We only knew him and Mrs Phillimore in his retirement during which he completed and published the official history of the Survey, though he had some difference with government as to the definition of sections of the frontier with Tibet. He died at Gulmarg in 1969 and was buried in the little cemetery there among the pines.

Today in Britain the one to twenty-five thousand and one to fifty-thousand OS maps of Britain are a wonderful guide to mountain walkers or countryside explorers. For the rest proper maps are unknown, their place taken by sat navs or small-scale motoring atlases, fit only to guide those who hurry along motorways from one conurbation to another, often oblivious of the history, the detail of landscape or the fauna and flora of the land. Their place has been taken by the photographic surveys of Google, which even shows my car in our forecourt.

But maps: whether the sheets of the Ordinance Survey or the Survey of India, keys to route finding, as to the very nature and history of a landscape: these remain my favourite reading.

14
THE LAST OF THE ANCIENT BRITONS

I only recount memories of a few of the more notable of the slowly diminishing band, now long vanished, of British and European residents who stayed on in Kashmir after 1947. In one sense, as far as the School was concerned, we were the last of them.

Colonel and Mrs Phillimore wintered in Dehra Dun and travelled up by easy stages to Srinagar, to Nedou's Hotel, on 15 April each year before going on to their summer quarters at Hut 76, Gulmarg, on 15 May. In September they came down again to Nedou's and thence to Dehra Dun the following month. Hut 76 was among the few to have survived unscathed from the 'raiders' of 1947, the Pathans who had so nearly seized the Valley for Pakistan. Or was it only the Pathans? Rumour had it that it was the locals who had quietly removed the contents of many huts, wooden cottages in an older English style, and that the village houses around Tangmarg at the foot of the forest still contained Victorian china and furnishings. Invited to tea, we and our small children would arrive on foot or by pony to be greeted by a servant equal in age and dignity to the Phillimores. Their strawberry or raspberry jam, sometimes a little musty, was made from the berries growing nearby.

Colonel Phillimore, as already mentioned. had been Deputy Surveyor General of India. On one occasion I had taken Rod Sinclair, a young man who was helping in the

School, to visit him in Nedou's Hotel. Rod's father was a general, and before coming to Kashmir, he had just been to the Queen's Birthday Parade. 'Ah yes', mused the Colonel, 'the last time I was there it was the Old Queen.' He was revered by the Army unit at Gulmarg, and it was they who, after the funeral, finally informed us of his death. His request was to be buried in the little cemetery on the edge of the *marg* looking to the mountains. Though it had already been closed to be 'returned to nature', it seemed fitting that he should be placed there as its final occupant. The Indian Army provided a guard of honour. It somehow seemed right that they should thus honour the last passing figure of what had been a vast empire, the Last Post echoing back from the four thousand feet mountain wall above him.

Polly Lodge, whom our children referred to as the Last of the Ancient Britons, was the daughter of a Devonshire clergyman, and had first come to India as a lady's companion. For many years she had a slowly declining business as a hairdresser for visitors in the front room of her boat, moored on the river just above the post office. Our daughter was fascinated by 'Aunty Polly', especially by the wig and the illustrated 'Eugene Diploma 1912' which greeted us on entry. Polly had the quality, kindness and reserve of her background and one could imagine her growing up in a Devon vicarage over a century ago. She was almost transparently thin, with a mass of white hair. One Halloween a children's party was held on the roof of another elderly friend's houseboat on Nagin Lake, Polly being a guest. We sat under a full moon looking out over the water, playing pumpkin games while Polly, her hair streaming in the breeze, looked like an ancient goddess. At ninety-four she began to fail, and was taken to Scotland by a slightly younger friend. She pined for Kashmir and returned briefly before being taken back once more.

The Nedou family had set up hotels: Flashman's in Lahore, Faletti's in Rawalpindi and Nedou's in Srinagar and Gulmarg. They were kindly and redoubtable Austrian Protestants, a Miss Nedou still working in the sixties as a missionary in Maharashtra. Mr Willy Nedou still ran the Srinagar hotel. Loved by his staff, he was a help to anyone in need. Once a year he gave a tea party for the slowly diminishing band of foreign residents. As Chairman of the Srinagar and Gulmarg Cemeteries Committee, his generous donations enabled us to continue to repair the walls and pay the *mali*. There was also a Muslim branch of the family. Willy's brother Wally, who had died before our time, had broken a leg while skiing above Gulmarg as a young man, and had been cared for by *gujars*. He fell in love with their daughter, and became a Muslim to marry her. Their son Benjie inherited the Gulmarg hotel, and their daughter grew up to marry Sheikh Abdullah, outliving him to the year 2000. Begum Abdullah, or Polly as she was known in her younger days, was a resourceful support to him throughout his life.

Mr Johansen was a special friend who came to us for Christmas dinner over many years. Jo was a trader, importing pharmaceuticals and exporting varied Kashmir goods. He had left his native Denmark in 1906, was in Vladivostok at the time of the Russian Revolution, and traded through China, Turkestan and Mongolia for over thirty years. His company's outlet to the south was through Kashmir and he had landed up in Srinagar about 1950 when the Karakoram passes closed after the Chinese communist victory. He had a touchingly naïve appreciation of the communists, believing that they had cut the root of human selfishness in forbidding the bequest of land. However, I especially remember one conversation in which he spoke of the Chinese. He said, 'Of all the people who have thought of themselves as superior to others: the Brahmins, the Nazis, the British in India, none compare to the Chinese. They simply know that they are the civilised ones and all the rest of us are all barbarians. I cannot think of a worse fate for any nation than to be ruled by the Chinese.'

Jo was a man of principle and valued his pharmaceutical business as he could keep prices steady in times of scarcity such as when the road closed, knowing that otherwise the poor would be exploited. Sadly, as Biscoe used to say, 'Honesty is the best policy, but not yet in Kashmir.' One of Jo's trusted employees, as his master began to grow old and forgetful, detached his best agencies one by one and transferred them to a rival company he had set up while continuing in Johansen and Company's service. Jo was finally declared bankrupt and most of his scanty belongings were taken. He lived on in the draughty old house on Exchange Road with only a bed and a chair, and one aged servant.

The story has a happier ending. Mrs Naqshband, the Danish wife of the Chief Conservator of Forests, mentioned his plight to the Danish Ambassador, who came up and found that he was unaware of his right to a state pension. 'But I left Denmark in 1906,' said Jo. 'Never mind, you are a Dane,' replied the Ambassador. Jo ended his days in modest comfort.

15
INTELLIGENCE?

You can take a person out of Intelligence, but not Intelligence out of the person, or so it is said.

I was totally surprised when, just before getting my green beret at the end of the Royal Marines Young Officers' Commando Course in 1952, my friend Alan and I were called aside and siphoned off into the world of MI6. As anything I write has already been made public in the Secret War Exhibition at the Imperial War Museum, our promise of secrecy must be extraneous. We were inducted into various bits of training which was never put to use. I still have a well-thumbed copy of the Foreign Office manual *The Theory and Practice of Communism*, and recall the night when, as if in an occupied city and provided with the necessary information, we were caused to stick some mock plastic explosive in the generators of an oil refinery on Southampton Water. The directors of the refinery knew all about our games, we were informed, but the guards did not - and nor did their dogs.

At the end of National Service, after twenty interesting months in Austria, I was offered a five year contract. Would I have found myself, rather like John le Carré, a junior officer in some Central European Embassy? And where would that have led? A different offer, to start Expedition Training at Gordonstoun, came at the same time. I chose it - at a fraction of the salary - and have no regrets.

So was that brief immersion out of character? Perhaps not. At University I had, to my bafflement, been known to some as Old Mac - short for Machiavelli. Was I really so devious? Then later, as Unofficial Correspondent (Honorary Consul) for Kashmir to the UK High Commission in Delhi, I was at the lowest and least noticeable end of what could be a useful chain of information. Kashmir being the secretive place it is, I guess it was also necessary to have a sixth sense of things happening around one, to keep one step ahead of the next impossible situation. Though I had earlier lived happily in Pakistan, yet, seeing the increased influence of a radical minority willing to use terror in the name of religion, I was profoundly glad to serve within an India which was still a secular democratic state.

Seen from our street level viewpoint in Muslim Central Asia the stock of Britain and 'the West' plummeted with the coincident arrival of the Hippies ('White Trash') and the Saudis tripling the price of oil. Yet Britain still behaved as an Imperial power, using Muslims as pawns in her game. From my lowly unofficial perch I wrote to Mrs Thatcher, saying she should not be sending Hekmatyar weapons to defeat the Russians - who were anyway crumbling. He would come back to bite us. He did.

Then, living in Small Heath in Birmingham, culture shocked at the open acceptance of bad practice and undeserved privilege by self-styled 'community leaders', I sent to government in 1994 a single sheet detailing early signs of trouble among encapsulated Muslim communities in the inner city. This and other warnings were only recognised in 2014 - twenty years later - when my name was listed in a parliamentary report at the head of a very short list of those who had sought to warn government of the dangers in UK of accommodating in Birmingham Schools the 'Jamaat i Islami' politicised tenancy within an uncomprehending multicultural Britain.

So is this an anti-Muslim diatribe? Not at all!

Having lived happily and securely in a Muslim city for 25 years, and with Muslim friends at all levels, one sees the 'other side' all too clearly. In Birmingham the girls who are totally covered up in Sparkbrook are the flip side of those wearing almost nothing, clubbing on Broad Street. Terror killing is simply evil: but one can sympathise with ordinary Muslim parents who do not wish their daughters to follow the post-feminist attitudes blazoned across the world by a young American singer, much as we might love her songs and admire her courage.

The intelligence community has long been open to penetration by the 'other side' for when one gets close to real people, though they may represent 'the enemy' one finds we are all the same in so many ways.

Perhaps the clue is among the poor, those who suffer? When the West, which has tried to banish death and suffering, seeks a way of defeating the enemy without pain to itself, it deploys drones. Those familiar fortified farmsteads in Pakistan's Frontier province may well house Taliban fighters. They also house women and children, marriage parties and all the living of a joint family. So today, if terror attacks herald a new and awful war, we should not be surprised.

The secret to recovering our common humanity may be among the poor who are hungry, who suffer, and yet are strong.

In Srinagar, as Head of a famous school, I knew everyone: parents, old students, servants, neighbours: very rich and very poor. Some of my warmest memories are of the School servants, working long hours for little pay, good humoured, loyal, willing to do anything demanded for the common good. In the pages of my life, the memory of Yaqub Shah the leper stands out as a sign of human courage and resourcefulness. Among peoples like the nomadic *bakarwals*, as earlier in the Highlands of Scotland, one has known a kind of human fellowship which travelling in the mountains somehow rekindles and stimulates.

I have not been poor and have not suffered, having known few sorrows in my life; but I have long known those who have and who do. It may be from poverty or sickness, or for their faith, their politics or their ethnicity. No rational person chooses suffering, yet in an imperfect world it may be necessary.

Jonathan Sacks in *Not in God's Name* recounts how, meeting Holocaust survivors, he finds they have left anger and revenge behind them. In considering religion, he notes how the Western world changed when its religion came to crisis point in the sixteenth century. For the Jews, as the Romans finally began the attack to destroy the troublesome city of Jerusalem in AD 70, it was the savage *intra* Jewish killing in the beleaguered city that led to the end of their whole religious system. In Western European Christianity it was the time from 1520 to 1650, when Catholic and Protestant killed each other over their understanding of the mode of Christ's presence in the Eucharist, which led on to the (real!) Enlightenment and so via Nietzsche to today's broken down culture. In Islam, beyond the fight with the 'Empire' of the materialist West, it is the *intra* Muslim struggle at root whose pains afflict us all and whose outcome for 'Islam' the world must wait.

So much for "God". This is not a 'religious' book, though it challenges the religious illiteracy of the materialist West. But in looking at the faiths, one need go no further than the Shia of Islam or the reformed Hinduism of the Sikhs, let alone the suffering and triumph at the heart of my own faith, to understand that the battle is not always won by the biggest, the richest, the Trumps of the world. That is why Jesus, sending his followers out into the enemy's kingdom, said they should be harmless as doves but also wise as serpents. Seeking the welfare of all in a dangerous world, that could be a good watchword, and the secret of 'intelligence'.

16

WHY WERE WE THERE AND WHAT WAS THE MISSION?

This is a postscript to a little book on Kashmir, particularly thinking of the good times when we were there all those years ago, and especially meant for our old students at Biscoe and Mallinson. Beyond them some of it will interest others who wish to think back to that very different age. As you will have read, this isn't in any way a 'religious' book: it is mainly just pictures of the people and places we knew and loved. But we were missionaries, so this postscript is an attempt to say what that means in my understanding, in the setting of the School and of Kashmir, and to explain what we aimed for and how we came to be living at the back of Lal Chowk for that quarter century. I am writing it as a thank-you for the huge trust and affection we have known from all of you and because of your continuing invitations. I can't keep up on Facebook or Linkedin, so a book must do instead!

Just recently, over thirty years after leaving Srinagar, three good reminders of Kashmir have come. One is a warm invitation from an Old Boy to stay with him in Dubai once again. I have such warm memories of the hospitality of Khurshid's delightful family after staying with them during our 2014 Old Boys' reunion. The second is a letter from another Old Boy, Dr Stenzin Namgyal in Zangskar and the third is a lengthy phone call over Christmas, with

three members of one family, speaking from South India, Chandigarh and Jammu in a call marvellously aided by technology.

Doctor Stenzin's letter takes me back in memory to a visit to Padum in 1984, before the road from Kargil over the Pensi La pass opened up that vast area to the world. I met the Rajah, an old gentleman and clearly poor, and found there was no schooling there. An offer of half fees for any boys who came to us from Zangskar was taken up, and the Rajah sent his grandson Stenzin and another lad, Phurboo. As a result, both are now doctors serving their own people in Zangskar and in Nubra, until recently most remote of Himalayan regions. Dr Stenzin writes from Padum of all the School had made possible for him.

Thirdly, over Christmas we had a lengthy phone call from Jag Mohan Sharma, 'Best All Round Boy' in 1970, and his wife and daughter, with whom we stayed in 2012, and who has so remarkably served both Kashmir and then the whole of India in the vital sphere of electrical power supply, and whose long friendship is important to us. Think of it, his role is to bring light where there is darkness, on a vast scale!

It is a matter of deep reflection, to hold together such relationships with life experience which has led me to increasing assurance in the reality—in spite of appearances to the contrary—of God's active and growing presence in today's world. That is part of the thinking behind this book. By His presence I mean the increase of people and communities across the world where genuine love and its fruit in the care and practical blessing of all, especially the poor and oppressed, spreads and deepens. In the present world there is inevitably also such darkness, pain and hatred: but that is finally the losing side. Christians are not alone in believing that in the end God's love and justice will be all in all. They are distinctive in the faith that his love is uniquely focussed in the life, execution, resurrection and ascension of Jesus two thousand years ago, and that it is His Spirit, even sometimes not recognised, which is present to motivate us today and to bring change. I have seen enough of faithful people who hold other faiths to know—and there is plenty of support for this in my scriptures — that God has no favourites. We shall all have surprises!

Students often generously remember their old School and Principal, just as I still remember my own schooling at Caterham in the Surrey hills, and all the good adventures of boyhood in those wartime years of the 1940s. But how did it come about that I should find myself Principal of such a school as Tyndale Biscoe, and how should a young Englishman, well after the days of the British Empire, land in Kashmir? We seemed to 'fit' the place, and it 'fitted' us so well. Was this all a matter of chance? What was the preparation? Perhaps I should try to explain. One should first confess: anyone who knows my wife knows I could have done little without her, so there was also the question of her very different route to Srinagar.

Before arriving there in January 1962, I had taught at Lawrence College in the Murree Hills of Pakistan on a three-year contract with the British Council as a housemaster. Before that I had started Expedition Training and taught History at Gordonstoun, a school well known for its links to the British royal family. Its founder, Dr Kurt Hahn, has a significant place in the history of education, linked with his own courageous stand against the rise of Hitler in Germany. He appointed me because he wanted to include leadership training and experience of the mountains as well as seamanship in his school. He believed they were vital in the building of character. I already had, at university and during military service with the Royal Marine Commandos, seven years' experience of the mountains, and of strong relationships with small groups of companions formed in hard places. Amazingly, Hahn—and thus his school—had a close and formative link with Canon Tyndale Biscoe, though I did not learn the nature of the connection until after we left Kashmir in 1986. Yet when I made a brief visit to Sheikh Bagh in 1960, I had a strange sense that I had seen it all before. There was somehow a family likeness to what I had known at Gordonstoun. I felt it was the place where we were meant to be.

While at Gordonstoun I had absolutely no thought of moving overseas, to Kashmir or anywhere else. My passion was adventure, and I loved the camaraderie of staff and boys in the mountains, in Scotland or even in the Swiss Alps. In 1956 five of us, young teachers, formed a plan to go the following year to the Karakoram, to explore a peak near Ishkoman, west of Gilgit. Meantime that summer vacation, three of us were to climb above Arolla in Switzerland. The first day out something happened which was so significant for me that I have referred to it at the beginning of this book. That day we were to acclimatise, nothing very hard, climbing on a ridge above the valley. I had a bad stomach, so after struggling up through the forest, finding I was holding the others back, I told them to go on while I went back. In the evening Jo returned saying, 'Andy's fallen!' A mass of rock had split off and carried him down several hundred feet, crushing him and killing him instantly.

Andy was very special. By far the best climber among us, he had left Gordonstoun to teach at Anavryta, a linked school in Athens. He had also spent time helping young people in the Gaza Strip, even then a place of conflict and suffering. I had been involved in accidents before, but none of them had touched me as this did. I felt shattered. My cosy life was as broken as his crushed body. As Andy's father and

Mr Chew our Headmaster came to Arolla for his funeral I remember blurting out a kind of unspoken prayer, 'God, if there is a God, why did Andy die?'

Four of us were still planning to go to Ishkoman, and I was tasked with getting maps and a liaison officer. It was just nine years after Partition, and a Scottish officer was still Commandant at the Pakistan Military Academy. He was related to one of our staff. I wrote to Brigadier Soutar and he replied saying he could help. He also said that a friend of his was Principal of Lawrence College and wanted someone to teach English and as a housemaster. Would any of us be interested? I had a rather confused sense that Andy's death should not be wasted, and said, 'I'm going.'

The British Council underwrote a contract and so I arrived in the Murree Hills, for the first time outside Europe, for what was to be a life changing three years. The first half was hard as I was out of my depth in a very different culture. When Mr Flecker fell sick and left soon after my arrival I was the only foreigner on the staff. In my boarding house of fifty boys I had no problems, but in class I made the mistake of being too friendly too quickly, and some of the boys from other houses took advantage and started joking in Punjabi across the class, so I lost control. After the close companionship of colleagues at Gordonstoun I was lonely. The night Martial Law was declared the Bursar ran away to his village, and in the morning the staff, who had well known that he was looting the College, were laughing. Their laughter horrified me, as in Britain anger would be their response. I began to understand financial corruption in a new way. I was suddenly in a world that was very strange to me, and I felt very alone.

There were cultural lessons, and I learnt them the hard way. Many of the boys were Pathans, for whom, once a guest is accepted, he is yours for three days. One day I was informed that a German scoutmaster had arrived. Would I like to accommodate him? A strange figure, with tatters of scout uniform, one leg, crutches and a patch over one eye, appeared at the head of a trail of wondering boys. I welcomed him in, then went off to teach. Returning an hour later, he was sitting on the balcony surrounded by boys. Every sentence echoed hatred of Jews and I was told the Head Boy was collecting all-round the College for him. He was no scoutmaster but an unrepentant Nazi, begging his way round the world.

Mr Muinuddin the Acting Principal told me to get rid of him and to say that if he took any money, the police would be informed. As I saw him off through the pine trees, he called out that it was because I was English, and he was German. I was booed by the whole College as I went in to lunch, and the contents of the lavatory were pushed through my door.

Nevertheless, it wasn't all bad. I received great hospitality from several families and made some good trips with boys into the mountains of Swat and the Kaghan Valley. The staff were friendly, and I began to learn something of the history and culture, of the area and the people. I was made welcome and stayed in places as widely different as the Northern Scouts mess in Gilgit and Aitchison College in Lahore. There I stayed with Major Geoffrey Langlands, who stayed on in Pakistan as a much loved and notable teacher, and who died only recently aged a hundred and one. I received hospitality from parents in Swat, Sialkot and Peshawar. Much was good, but somehow, I was needing something more, without knowing quite what it was.

Geoffrey Bingham had been a sergeant in the Australian Army in 1941 when the Japanese entered the war. He was decorated for bravery, severely wounded and taken prisoner, enduring four years in Changi Jail, Singapore. It was an experience which either made, or broke, men. In 1958 he was living with his wife three miles away up in Murree, looking after the children of missionaries. I got to know him, a man in a thousand. On one occasion he came down for a meal and after a good evening I insisted on accompanying him on the long walk back up to Murree. Over the last mile he needed some support. His leg had never fully recovered from the war injury. I began to think, 'What kind of man is this who accepts an invitation involving such a trek, knowing he would find it hard to get home?' There was clearly something in the faith that Geoff had and that I very much needed.

I took down the Bible that had been unread since it had been given to me on leaving school thirteen years earlier, and it led me, quite simply, to meeting Jesus.

I say quite simply. It was in fact a long and repeated reading of the gospels and the letters of St Paul in an easy to read version, a slow recognition that it all, somehow, made sense of the world and of me. It became clear that it involved a response to his promise to invite 'Jesus' into my life. This I did as a prayer, and my world began to change, though I could not at that moment see how it would happen. I think and hope I didn't, then or since, become overly 'religious' in the conventional sense. We easily forget that the main enemies of Jesus were the leaders of his own religion, and his friends were so often ordinary 'sinners', women, the poor and those of religions and races other than his own. Positive faith somehow all hinged on coming into relationship with him. I think that coming to know Jesus is the single most important thing that can happen in anyone's life. It happened to Biscoe as a Cambridge student, and through him, it changed so much in Kashmir. It can happen to anyone, regardless of religion or condition.

The second half of my three years in Pakistan was very different from the first. Relationships in the school changed out of all recognition as I found I could welcome some of the difficult pupils, and was, at a tricky juncture, asked to take over as Senior House Master (Discipline). Of course, I was also getting accustomed to the culture of Pakistan and enjoying much of it.

Geoff Bingham was that mysterious thing, a missionary. He certainly hadn't preached to me but had been a friend when I needed a friend. Over the following weeks I met others who came up to Murree to gain language skills. Among these was Catherine McHardy, a young Edinburgh-trained Scottish doctor preparing to work in the rural hospital at Jalalpur Jattan. She had had a settled intention to serve God overseas from her teenage years. Our courtship caused ample interest, both among the Lawrence College students and in the mission community. When we announced our engagement, the College sought to enrol her whenever they could. She helped dress *The Merchant of Venice* and, Mr Muinuddin's wife being unwell, coped as hostess to a meeting of the Pakistan Public Schools Association.

I had, during my first year in Pakistan, met Dr Phil Edmonds, who after leaving Biscoe in 1955 had gone to Edwardes College, Peshawar. He had expressed great interest in Dr Hahn and Gordonstoun and now wrote, 'Are you thinking of being a missionary, and would you consider whether God wants you at Tyndale Biscoe?' The answer to the first question was 'no'. I was happily and usefully engaged at Lawrence College. As to the second question, in the recesses of my mind I had heard something of an extraordinary Victorian missionary, Tyndale Biscoe, who had done astonishing social work in the city of Srinagar. I determined to find out more.

In the following winter holiday, I went across that awkward border between Lahore and Amritsar and flew up to Kashmir. The Biscoe School was something of an orphan at the time, its wooden fences rotting, and five Principals having come and gone in eight years. Yet meeting some of the local staff, all old students of the School, and all I heard and read, confirmed a sense of a definite family resemblance to Gordonstoun. How could that be? In any event it also confirmed in my mind a sense of 'calling' to go there. It was not just 'chance'.

The rest, as they say, is history. The Bishop of Amritsar, Tyndale Biscoe's Chair of Governors, wanted us, and the Church Missionary Society accepted me after not very extensive training. Catherine they gladly welcomed from the Church of Scotland. Thus, married in her home church in Edinburgh in 1961, we duly arrived in Lal Chowk in January 1962.

One has to say that it was the tragedy of Andy's death that propelled me to Pakistan for that essential three years' real preparation for responsibility in Kashmir. But it was meeting Jesus that made a 'missionary', little though at that time I understood the implication of the term. All 'chance'?

As for the link between the School and Gordonstoun, that I discovered much later. There were a number of outstanding, and often controversial, missionaries in Victorian times. Tyndale Biscoe was one. Another, who went first to Trinity College, Kandy, Ceylon (now Sri Lanka) was a Scotsman, the Rev AG Fraser. He then went on to West Africa to the Gold Coast (now Ghana) to found Achimota School. In both places he did an extraordinary work. Very early he had heard of Biscoe's impact in Kashmir, and in 1913 travelled the length of India to meet him. He was overwhelmed by what he saw in the Fateh Kadal school and then wrote, 'It makes me ashamed of my work at Trinity, ashamed.' Becoming famous for his work in both Asia and Africa, he met Dr Hahn at some point around 1935 when he became the first Principal of a College of Adult Education in Scotland. There he grew into an intimate friendship with Hahn, who persuaded him to become his first Chaplain at the Outward-Bound School at Aberdovey and then in 1945 at Gordonstoun. It was Aberdovey from which the Duke of Edinburgh's Award sprang, with its threefold emphasis on service, crafts or skills and testing adventure. It is known in India as the IYA, the International Youth Award.

Fraser was clearly among those who by the quality and nature of their lives deeply influenced Hahn. Biscoe was one who undoubtedly had a considerable impact on Fraser. However it happened, there were clear echoes of Hahn and of Gordonstoun when I first met the legacy of Tyndale Biscoe in Kashmir. It has been one of my privileges to follow, in a different age, in the footsteps of both of them.

That may explain how and why we found ourselves in Srinagar. It leaves the more important question: 'What is the mission?'

For me, however much I may have failed, it has centred around slowly built relationships with boys, especially in the mountains, just because that is something I can do. Other people have quite different gifts, maybe as scientists, in business or as carpenters or bus drivers, but it is their human relationships that are often the key. I had come to the start of knowing Jesus though a relationship, a friendship, with Geoff Bingham who was already very clearly a friend of Jesus. Jesus says to his followers, 'I have called you friends.' My realisation that that could apply to me, which began to become real for me at the age of thirty-one, is slowly refining my life. How can one pass on such a relationship across the barriers of age, race, religion and any other?

It is not, as is commonly thought, only a question of religious belief, but also of experience. Having closely observed matters of faith, religion and the world's political and social life for long enough, I feel sure that the truth, affirmed in at least two of the world's religions, that Jesus is alive, and is coming back to set everything right, is central to God's purposes. And his friends have the privilege of seeing how He is already, unseen by the world, ushering in that good Kingdom of love, justice and freedom from fear and death.

I have been witness to that, both in Kashmir and more recently in Birmingham. I hope, after the present small book, to write something more on our twenty-eight years in one of the world's truly multi-cultural cities.

We live in an age of great violence and suffering, but when there are also new avenues of hope and freedom. The internet gives new freedoms to all to use for good or evil. One of my expectations drawn from observations of young people in the Pakistani community in Birmingham, especially women, is that as many appeal to scripture, often against cultural norms, they will search in both Quran and Bible for all that is written of Jesus.

What may appear to many people as chance, blind fate, can also be experienced as the invisible hand guiding every detail of our lives as we seek to 'love God and love our neighbour'. That's my hope in writing for many friends in Kashmir or scattered across the world, just as I hope you have enjoyed the stories and word pictures of the Kashmir we knew in those good years.

There is no doubt that our schools began to change Kashmir in the times, and especially through the lives, of CE Tyndale Biscoe and Miss Mallinson. It is quite possible that this can happen again, at a time when Kashmir urgently needs new hope, if some of our young people catch a vision of how God is in the business of changing society for the better, and how He actually uses us imperfect humans to help Him. A warning: it is one thing to catch a vision; it is quite another matter to follow it through. That needs persistent faith and hard work, 'to struggle in the open field until the end of time', in the words of Lesslie Newbigin. If one has a sense of God's providential leading, it can be something of a roller coaster, a wonderful lifelong adventure. When people tell me, 'You've had an interesting life,' I reply, 'I'm still having an interesting life.' Join the party!

AFTERWORD

I met John Ray in a most unusual way. In 1960 I hitch-hiked from London to India via Turkey, Iran and Pakistan. After a week in Lahore I decided to hitch to Kabul and went to a government health clinic for a typhoid vaccination. An American nurse who worked at a mission hospital was there. Was she a missionary? She wore white cotton socks, a wide flower printed cotton skirt, a clean, pressed, white cotton blouse and no jewellery or make-up, nor did she dye her hair. Everything about her seemed worthy and decent. Having never met a missionary before, I sounded my belief about Religion. 'Fundamentally,' I said, 'all religions are the same.'

'You don't know your Bible,' she replied sweetly.

Didn't know the Bible? What presumption! Both of my grandfathers had been church elders, and my maternal grandmother had been a Sunday School teacher for over thirty years. (She was forever quoting aphorisms from the Book of Proverbs.) My parents took us to Sunday School every Sunday, and I knew all the stories, having heard them over and over: Noah and the Flood, Joseph and his Coat of Many Colours, David and Goliath, John the Baptist dressed in camel hair and a leather belt preaching in the desert and feeding on locusts and 'wild' honey, the Wisemen whom a star led to Bethlehem, baby Jesus in the manger, Jesus astounding the rabbis with his precocious teaching, Jesus walking on water, Jesus on the Cross. There were always prayers at bedtime ('Bless Mummy and Daddy...'), grace before all meals ('May the Lord make us truly grateful and bless this food which we are about to receive')—what did I *not* know about the Bible?

She suggested that I go to Murree, a hill station in Azad (Free) Kashmir[3] where missionaries went during the summer months 'for 'fellowship' and to strengthen their Urdu.

'You will find some people there who can help you,' she said.

The road leaving Lahore for Kabul was the same that I had taken cycling to Jahangir's Tomb and the Badshahi Masjid. I soon caught a lift as far as Islamabad, Pakistan's new capital, where the Mahabharata was first recited, Rawalpindi, a green city in a dry land like Lahore, and on to Peshawar and Kabul.

I hitch-hiked back three days later.

The sun set over Attock Fort and when I reached Peshawar they were celebrating the Eid al-Adha, the Muslim feast day commemorating Abraham's offer to sacrifice his son, Isaac. The streets were ablaze with bonfires and musicians singing to the throb of tom-toms. I crossed the Indus and hitch-hiked all night. Alighting from a lorry near Rawalpindi next morning shortly after dawn, I saw a road sign, 'Murree 20 miles', and remembered the nurse in Lahore who suggested that I go there to meet missionaries and learn 'with their help' something about the Bible. Why not? Despite losing my Christian faith at university, religion continued to interest me as a 'subject' alongside art, music, literature, history and philosophy in the curriculum of a broad education. Yet I had not read the Bible or had not heard it discussed as an adult and was unable to answer intelligently when Muslims questioned me about it. Murree

---

3   The sector of pre-Partition Kashmir in what was then West Pakistan.

was *only* twenty miles, the distance between Bay St Louis, where we had lived during my childhood, and Gulfport. Overlooking India and the hills falling away to the Vale of Kashmir, it might be an agreeable place to study. It was a Sunday morning, and finding missionaries there would be easy: they would be at church, and I had only to wait outside until the service ended. I would go with the flow, I decided, leave it up to Fate. I would lift a thumb for *every* vehicle, whether bound for Lahore or Murree and take the first car or lorry that stopped for me.

A Murree-bound car appeared almost at once, and the driver stopped for me.

Murree was then little more than a village but had two Protestant churches, formerly Church of Scotland and Church of England; now both Church of Pakistan. I found one easily and waited. The service ended. However, none of the missionaries evinced the least interest in me, nor why should they? Evangelising was their *job*, and they were on holiday. The moment after service was reserved for 'fellowship' with cherished friends and colleagues, not for professing the Gospel to hobos. Had some exuberant Lawrence College[4] students not intercepted me leaving town, my Murree project would have ended there. They

---

4   Lawrence College was founded in 1960 by Sir Henry Lawrence for the Anglo-Indian community and, until 1960, comprised both girls' and boys' schools and a teacher training section. Games fields were carved out of the hillside. Staff cottages were sprinkled up and down the small lanes and a fine stone-built neo-Gothic chapel stood on the ridge at the top. It is about 6,000 feet above sea level and 1,000 feet and three miles below Murree, a hill station on the old road to Kashmir from the railhead at Rawalpindi. By 1947 the Anglo-Indian staff had left and were replaced by Punjabi Muslims, and by 1957 the boys were mainly sons of Army officers and zamindars. Most were Punjabis, but a fair number were Pathans.

wanted me to meet their teacher from England. 'Pleeeze, sirrrr, it is only one furlong, isn't it?' When I assented, a dispute as to who was to carry my rucksack erupted.

Thus I came to meet a little man with bushy eyebrows who stood in the back door of his house and glared down at me. 'What do you want?' he demanded almost ferociously. A German 'scoutmaster'. a Long John figure with one leg, a patch over one eye and wearing tattered fragments of scout uniform, had appeared at Lawrence College recently, collected Rps. 450 from students organised by the Prefects, bade goodbye by dumping retaliatory excrement through his letter box as punishment for opposing the collection, and gone on his way, presumably to the next school. My torn shirt and frayed jeans were sufficient proof: I was another mendicant, another confidence trickster.

My response surprised him. It surprised me, for, weighing all retrospectively, I believe the words were not of my own crafting. 'I have come to learn something about Christianity.' Had I said, 'Mr Ray, you have won the Lottery,' and presented him with a million pounds, the galvanising effect could not have been stronger. I do not reconstruct his response. I recall his precise words. 'Come in,' he said. '*Kansaman* (the cook) is not here today. It's his day off. But help yourself to anything you want and stay as long as you want.' Then, leading me to his study through *Kansaman*'s kitchen, he selected a book from a small library there and said, 'You might start with this. Don't read it verse by verse. Read it as you would a novel.' Providing a pen and pad, he added, 'Note any questions you have, and, if I can't answer them, I will find you someone who can.'

The book that he selected was J.B. Phillips' *Letters to Young Christians*,[5] a modern translation of the Epistles. The

---

5   London: Geofrey Bles, 1960.

translator believed that the Epistles (letters) were written hurriedly in vernacular Greek to ordinary men about specific problems concerning their faith.

Reading them as ordinary letters allowed me to consider the words in their plain meaning. Each letter contained a salutation, a touch of news and a valediction. Each showed a concern for those to whom it was addressed. The letters' authors were not mythological icons, but real people who, history demonstrated, had given over their lives to their belief, and the experiences they described were real.

'We are writing to you about something which has always existed, yet which we ourselves actually saw and heard, something which we had opportunity to observe closely and even to hold in our hands, and yet, as we know now, was something of the very word of life himself. For it was life which appeared before us: We saw it, we are eye-witnesses of it, and are now writing to you about it,' proclaimed John's First Epistle.[6]

I found what I believed was the crux of Christian doctrine, Man's incapacity to live a moral life without God's help, in Paul's Letter to the Romans.

Paul tells us that he had always *known* what was right but was unable to live a righteous life.

'My own behaviour baffles me. For I find myself not doing what I really want to do but doing what I really loathe.[7]... I often find that I have the will to do good, but not the power. That is, 1 don't accomplish the good I set out to do, and the evil I don't really want to do I find I am always doing[8]... In my mind I am God's willing servant, but in my own nature I am bound fast ... to the law of sin

---

6   1 John: 1:1.
7   Rom. VII.
8   Rom 7: 15-24.

and death.'[9] This conflict between Man's conscience and his servitude to sin, he concluded, 'is an agonising situation, but I thank God there is a way out, through Jesus... For the new spiritual principle of life "in" Christ Jesus lifts me out of the old vicious circle of sin and death.'[10]

'The word of God cuts more keenly than any two-edged sword,' I read in the Letter to Jewish Christians (Hebrews). 'It strikes through to the place where soul and spirit meet, to the innermost intimacies of a man's being. It exposes the very thoughts and motives of a man's heart.'[11] The Second Letter to Peter spoke of 'those who have indulged all the foulness of their lower natures and have nothing but contempt for authority.' Such men were 'arrogant and presumptuous ... they think nothing of scoffing at the glories of the unseen world.[12]... These are the men who delight in daylight self-indulgence; they are foul spots and blots, playing their tricks at your very dinner-tables. Their eyes cannot look at a woman without lust, they captivate the unstable ones, and their technique of getting what they want is, through long practice, highly developed. With their high-sounding nonsense they use the sensual pull of the lower passions to attract those who were just on the point of cutting loose from their companions in misconduct. They promise them liberty. Liberty! – when they themselves are bound hand and foot to utter depravity.' They were like 'wells without a drop of water in them' and 'the changing shapes of whirling storm-clouds'.[13] Man was 'the slave of whatever masters him'.[14] 'When all kinds of trials and temptations crowd into your

---

9   Rom 7:23.
10   Rom 7:15, 18-19, 23-24, 8:1-2.
11   Heb. 4:12.
12   2 Pet 2:10.
13   2 Pet 13-14, 17+19.
14   2 Pet 2: 17-20.

lives … don't resent them as intruders, but welcome them as friends!' wrote James. 'Realise that they come to test your faith and to produce in you the quality of endurance. But let the process go on until that endurance is fully developed, and you will find you have become men of mature character with the right sort of independence.'[15]

On finishing the Epistles, I moved on to the Gospels, the record of Christ's ministry, again in J.B. Phillips' translation. Matthew opened with a matter of fact statement about the Nazarene's ancestry: 'This is the record of the ancestry of Jesus Christ who was the descendant of both David and Abraham.'[16] John concluded in a similarly matter of fact way. 'Of course, there are many other things which Jesus did, and I suppose, if each one were written down in detail, there would not be room in the whole world for all the books that would have to be written.'[17]

The Interim pages were written as with fire.

'Jesus now moved about through the whole of Galilee, teaching in their synagogues and preaching the good news about the kingdom, and healing every disease and disability among the people. His reputation spread throughout Syria, and people brought to him all those who were ill, suffering from all kinds of diseases and pains—including the possessed, the insane and the paralysed. He healed them and was followed by enormous crowds from Galilee, the Ten Towns, Jerusalem, Judaea, and from beyond the river Jordan.'[18]

The Gospel writers were no mere hero worshippers, but, even if they were, why should they have singled out Jesus? Why should such an exalting story have been written

---

15   James 1:2-4.
16   Matt 1:1.
17   John 21:25.
18   Matt 4:23-25.

at all? Why had nothing of equal power been written? Why would a man of such gifts of perception, wisdom and powers of expression claim that he was the Son of God, if he was not? The man's life *was* unusual. And who could deny that his words had the ring of authority?

'Happy are those who are hungry and thirsty for goodness.'[19] 'Happy are the utterly sincere, for they will see God.'[20] 'The man who is faithful in the little things will be faithful in the big things, and the man who cheats in the little things will cheat in the big things too.'[21] 'The axe already lies at the root of the tree, and the tree that fails to produce good fruit will be cut down end thrown into the fire.'[22] 'Be on your guard against covetousness in any shape or form, for a man's real life in no way depends upon the number of his possessions.' 'The narrow gate and the hard road lead out into life, and only a few are finding it.'[23] 'He makes his sun rise upon evil men as well as good, and he sends his rain upon honest and dishonest men alike.'[24] 'Pray for those who persecute you.'[25] 'Do not pile up treasures on earth, where moth and rust can spoil them and thieves can break in and steal, for wherever your treasure is, you may be certain that your heart will be there too.'[26] 'Remember, there are things men consider perfectly splendid which are detestable in the sight of God.'[27] 'There is more joy in Heaven over one sinner whose heart is changed than over ninety-

---

19 Matt: 5:6.
20 Matt 5: 6-8.
21 Luke 16:10.
22 Matt 3:10.
23 Matt 6:19-21.
24 Matt 5:45.
25 Matt 5:45.
26 Matt 6:19:21.
27 Luke 16:15.

nine righteous people who have no need for repentance.'[28] 'Ah, if you only knew, even at this eleventh hour, on what your peace depends—but you cannot see it.'[29] 'The kingdom of heaven is inside you.'[30]

The days passed as the pages turned, and all about me swirled the facts about Jesus' life and teaching and the implications for mankind. John followed my progress with the avidity of a recent convert. I shudder to think now how fatuous my questions must have seemed to him, but he treated them all with patience, never once belittling me. Christianity, he said, was unlike other belief systems, in that it made promises that were fulfilled, as seen in various books in his collection describing the 'miracles' of changed lives, cured alcoholics and dope addicts, repaired marriages. Certainly it had changed his life. He no longer needed others' testimony; he had his own experience. He knew by personal experience the 'miracle' of a changed life. Christ had changed *his* life.

Our discussions degenerated at times into abstruse speculation. We were, after all, erstwhile Gordonstoun schoolmaster and lawyer.

C.S. Lewis' *The Screwtape Letters* led me to assert, for example, that Lewis' contention that Satan prevents us from believing in God was 'tautologous in that Satan presupposes belief in God'. The potential for endless debate from such premises is clear, and it is to John Ray's credit that he made a courteous exit. Had he persisted in this arid contest, he might have killed my interest in *Screwtape*. Paul imparts practical advice about disputation in Second Timothy. '(H)ave nothing to do with silly and ill-informed controversies

---

28   Luke 15:7.
29   Luke 20:42.
30   Luke 17:21.

which lead inevitably ... to strife... (T)he Lord's servant must ... have patience and the ability gently to correct those who oppose his message... must always bear in mind that God will give them a different outlook.'[31]

Much later, when I came to appreciate the difficulty of explaining rationally matters whose first principle is that they were beyond human reasoning, I re-read *Screwtape* and was able to understand Lewis' 'tautology' in Paul's terms of a conflict of good and evil. Why a principle of evil should be tolerated in a system reigned over by a loving God remained a mystery, but the conflict itself seemed to be an observable fact. 'God' and 'Satan' obviated the need for befuddling new jargon.

When John felt unable to provide a sufficient answer he referred me, as promised, to someone who could. Then we would walk up the hill together and pester the missionaries at the language school. A pretty Scottish doctor named Catherine was there improving her Urdu. One suspects that she afforded John an added incentive to walk up the hill.

Among the other remarkable people I met were an Anglican minister named Jim Hewitt, two English missionaries named Peter and Alison Bagnall and an Australian missionary named Geoffrey Bingham.

Jim Hewitt was very far from the type of evangelist who might grab you in a train and ask if you were 'saved'. A reticent, scholarly man by temperament, he had an ordered way of presenting his thoughts, first enumerating the steps in his argument, then calmly addressing each in turn. One of the most interesting conversations I have had in my life was a conversation with him occupying most of a long afternoon. Without belittling Islam, he delineated the differences between it and Christianity. The Qur'an for the Muslim, he explained, were Allah's *ipsissima verba* inscribed on tablets and

---

31   2 Tim 3:23-4.

transmitted by the angel Gabriel to Muhammad when he was in a trance. Muhammad recited them, and the words were recorded—hence *al-Qur'an* (the Recitation). They can suffer no abridgment, not even translation. Muslims memorise and use them in Arabic without always understanding what they mean—very different from the Christian's perception of revelation. To the Muslim Allah created the Earth and prescribed its physical and moral laws. He does not 'save' us. Man *earns* salvation either by dying for the Faith (*jihad*) or compliance with the Five Pillars. There is no remission of these laws, no Grace; salvation is formal and impersonal. The Christian perception of Revelation is very different. The Bible's words are those of ordinary men guided by God's holy spirit, as shown by his use of ordinary men to transmit his message to us. Hence its errors and inconsistencies. And hence the evolution of a tribal war god (Yahweh) demanding animal sacrifices to a universal God who offered himself as the sacrificial lamb. God hasn't changed. Human perception of God has changed. Salvation for the Christian is in the reciprocal exchange between divine Grace and fallible Man's response.

The notion that God's 'son' died by the hand of man to 'save' us is repugnant to the Muslim. Allah's prophets, moreover, are invulnerable.

Christ lived and taught at the confluence of three civilisations, the Greek, Roman and Hebrew. Jim Hewitt stressed this, as well as a point I had already taken, that Jesus' personal life exemplified his teachings. He did not disturb my respect for Islam, nor did he intend to. Indeed, he shared it. Jim Hewitt was first and forever a teacher, a missionary.

Geoffrey Bingham[32] was a wire haired 'Good on ya, no worries, mate' sort of bloke, whose lined face and battered

---

32 http://en.wikipedia.org/wiki/Geoffrey_Bingham.

features told of six years spent in a Japanese prisoner of war camp after the fall of Singapore. He had been a corporal in the Australian Army, held the Military Medal and had been recommended for the Victoria Cross. Despite a war wound that hadn't healed, he had worked his way through Moore Theological College in Sydney by wring short stories and after ordination wrote over forty books and commentaries on The Acts of the Apostles, Ephesians, Galations, John's Gospel, Mark's Gospel, 1 Peter, Philippians, Colossians, 1 Thessalonians, Ecclesiastes, The Revelation of St. John, The Song of Solomon, Titus and Romans. I spent another long afternoon with him. We walked to the top of a mountain, sat down under a tree and talked. 'Have you ever thought what the summary of the commandments must have been for the Jews?' he asked me. 'The Jews thought it was *their* Law which distinguished them from the heathen. To their caste system, their long robes adorned with inscribed parchments and their parading about declaiming "Eli! Eli!" Christ's reply to them quoting their Scriptures, was, "Love one another. Just as I have loved you"[33] and "I will have mercy, and not sacrifice!"[34] This gigantic thought, the paramountcy of Love, came into the world with Jesus. Is that a coincidence? All the ethical values the world now accepts as self-evident had their origin in Jesus. Man is capable of perfection. "Be ye therefore perfect, even as your Father who is in Heaven!"[35] We have watered this down, but that capacity for perfection is the significance of our creation in the image of God.'

Whether Peter Bagnall was inordinately curious about his friends' guests, perceived an evangelistic opportunity or was abnormally hospitable, I shall never know, but he

---

33   John 13:34. Matt 9:13.
34   Hosea 6:6.
35   Matt 5:48.

invited me to spend a night with his family as soon as we met and without first consulting his wife; then, turning to John, asked, 'What do you say, old stink? A capital idea?' He relished John's intense Englishness, always addressing him as 'old chap', 'old bean' or 'old stink'. Peter was an undergraduate at Cambridge when the Second World War started. He left Cambridge to join the Forces and was sent to India, where he saw action in the Battle of Imphal. He had a Christian conversion, and, when the war ended, stayed in India and worked as an itinerant evangelist, first in the eastern Himalayas around Darjeeling, then in Karachi. He stood in the bazaar reading his Urdu Bible waiting for someone to ask what he was reading. One question led to another, then he would read aloud passages where the Bible differed from the Qur'an. Muslims, he said, were particularly responsive to such an approach, as the Qur'an taught them to accept the authority of the Jewish and Christian scriptures. When his correspondent began to tire of the discussion, Peter appointed a time to meet later, and, so long as interest remained, continued his instruction, relying always on the Scriptures alone. His objective was to get his correspondent to read the Bible for himself. He did this for two years, then returned to Cambridge, took his degree, married and came out to Pakistan as a Church Missionary Society (CMS) missionary with a monthly salary of Rps.700/–[36], half of which, John told me, he spent on Bibles to give away.

I spent a day and a night with the Bagnalls. Managing a family with three children on £25 a month cannot have been easy for Alison Bagnall, and many women of her background in her position would have been resentful. I asked her whether she was not nostalgic for Cambridge, where they had lived before coming out to Pakistan. Cambridge

---

36 About £50 at the then current exchange rate.

had been a 'preparation', she replied. It was nice to go back on visits, but Pakistan was now their home. Pakistan was the place to which they had been 'called'. The simplicity of their material life, the joy evident in all they did, their unreserved submission to their perception of God's plan for them and hearing them through the wafer-thin walls of their cottage praying together made an enduring impression on me.

John Ray was a young man of thirty-two when we met in Murree. He married Catherine a year after I left Murree and was the headmaster of the Tyndale-Biscoe Mission School in Srinagar from 1962 until he left in 1986 for Birmingham to work with the Muslim community there. The Tyndale-Biscoe School's motto is 'In all things be men.' What was there in Jim Hewitt and Geoffrey Bingham that allowed them such gifts of perception and pedagogy? Why were Peter and Alison Bagnall so much happier with so much less? The pages turned, and the days passed—too regularly. Had it been within my power, I would have ordered the sun to stand still. John wanted me to stay on, but a fortnight was enough to impose on anyone. I took my leave one Tuesday afternoon after lunch, aware that his personal belongings were in the room where I had first read Jesus' words, but not yet aware that this had been the most important fortnight of my life. He gave me a small Bible to take with me and inscribed it with a passage from Zephaniah: 'The King of Israel, even the Lord, is in the midst of thee; thou shalt not see evil anymore.'[37]

I hope that missionary nurse I met in Lahore reads this. Her advice to visit Murree changed my life.

Shelby Tucker

---

37   Zephaniah 3:15.

GLOSSARY

Items are marked in the text in italic script

aloo	potato
astaan	a shrine
atta	whole wheat flour used to make *chapatis*
azadi	freedom
bakarwalsa	mostly-Sunni Muslim nomadic tribe based in the Pir Panjal and Himalayan mountains (they are mainly goatherds and shepherds)
baksheesh	a tip or a bribe
barat	a wedding procession
bearer	a domestic servant; a waiter and assistant cook
budmash	ruffian
bukhari	a wood burning stove with exhaust pipe often inserted in a small window pane
bund	raised river bank
chai	tea
chapati	traditional flat unleavened bread
charas	made from the resin of the cannabis plant
chowk	a broad open area where roads meet; commonly a market or meeting place
chenar	Oriental Plane, a large, deciduous tree growing to 100 feet or more, and knownfor its longevity and spreading crown
chulha	a small earthen or brick stove
chuprassi	a junior office worker who carries messages

Darbar	the Maharajah's Court
dustur / dustoor	custom or common practice
degchies	cooking pots
deg	huge cooking pots
djinn	spirit, often malevolent
dunga	a traditional wooden houseboat
Dussehra	a major Hindu festival
goguj	turnip
goondah	a ruffian; a hired thug
gujar	of a pastoral agricultural ethnic group, those in Kashmir being largely Muslim
gulley	in the city a narrow lane: in mountains a narrow steep defile
hoosh moosh	part of Kashmiri nature: rumour
kadal	a bridge
kahvaha	a sweet spicy tea
kangri	charcoal embers in an earthenware pot enclosed in a small basket for warming the body under the loose outer garment
karevas	plateaux above the level of the Valley of Kashmir representing earlier higher lake floors
khat/qat	a plant containing two main stimulant drugs which speed up mind and bod
khattak	a swift martial dance practised by Pathans Khuni Nallahliterally a 'bloody river bed'; a notorious landslip-prone spot on the Jammu route
khun	blood
kulcha	a tasty variety of seed-topped Kashmiri bread roll eaten with *chai*

kutch	a large traditional wooden boat used for carrying goods, poled upstream or tugged from a towpath
lathi	a long, heavy iron-bound bamboo stick used as a weapon, especially by police
lawas	a bubbly flat bread
mali	a gardener
marg	a mountain meadow
mohalla	an area of a town or village; a community
nallah	a small river
numbardar	a village headman who as the representative of a community of cultivators is responsible for the payment of their revenue
pagri	a turban of cloth bound round the head
Panch Ab	meaning five rivers; origin of the name Punjab
pandit	Kashmiri Brahmin
pheron	the traditional loose long-sleeved Kashmiri outer garment
Pir	a title for a Sufi master or spiritual guide
razai	a quilt
sag/saag	a curry of cooked of green leaves shalwar kamiz a traditional outfit of shirt and baggy trousers, designed differently for men and women
shikara	a type of small flat bottomed wooden boat found on the Dal Lake and other lakes and rivers
sweeper	a menial worker who attends to waste removal, bathroom sanitation and street sweeping, especially where modern piped water and WCs are non-existent
tehsildar	a minor revenue official and administrator
takht	a throne or seat of authority
tamasha	a spectacle

tiffin carriers	lunch tins
walla	suffix denoting a person who does a particular job or has a specific feature
wagoo	a traditional reed mat
zulam	oppression and cruelty

Acknowledgements

A number of people have demanded that I start writing. Among them are Shelby Tucker, author of *Among Insurgents* and long-time friend. I am grateful to him for enabling this UK edition, also for his afterword. Dr Jenny Taylor, friend and journalist, wants me to write about Birmingham. Steve Bell, long time inspirational National Director of Interserve UK, is a constant encouragement.

The Church Mission Society, which started the work in Kashmir back in the nineteenth century, faithfully supported us, both in Kashmir and for five years in Birmingham.

Ellora Rahi, who found time to bring an acute cultural sensitivity to the start of this book.

Jo Guy, my Cornish cousin, for encouragement and good advice

I could not have navigated the perils of publication without the keen co-operation of Ella Sonawane, Assistant General Secretary (Publishing & Mission) of ISPCK, right beside Kashmiri Gate in Delhi.

Without Catherine, wonderful wife of fifty-seven years (so far) there would have been no book, and by now no John Ray.